NAVIGATING

STRATEGY

A Practical Guide for Transforming Ideas into Reality

By Michael W. Beard

Simple Group Global

First Printing: 2018

ISBN 978-0692135761

Simple Group Global, LLC
United States of America

www.simplegroupglobal.com

NAVIGATING Strategy

Part of the NAVIGATING Business Series
by Simple Group Global

CONTENTS

SECTION 3:
PRACTICAL CONSIDERATIONS

FIGURES

HOW TO READ THIS BOOK

The Navigating Series is a collection of short practical books designed to guide you through our complicated global marketplace. Think of them as travel guidebooks to the great cities of the world. A guidebook helps you get the most out of your trip. At first, you skim through the book and map out what you want to do and see. Then, you go back and forth bookmarking places of interest that you want to explore further. Sometimes you even carry the guidebook with you so that you can read more about the places you decide to visit. Guidebooks are full of interesting facts, easy-to-read maps and helpful tips.

As the subtitle suggests, this is also a guidebook. The most useful way to approach this book is to sit down and read through it once quickly. It's short, so you should be able to finish it without a huge investment of time. Don't worry about catching everything the first time through. Go back over it again to bookmark any sections that you think will be immediately helpful to you. Then, read those sections more carefully. Finally, put some of the ideas presented in this book into practice. As the needs arise, you can return to relevant sections to make use of the information, tools and advice.

PREFACE

It takes as much energy to wish as it does to plan.

Eleanor Roosevelt

If you are confused about what a strategy is and when you might need one, then you're in the right place. This book is not written for MBA graduates or the CEOs of large multinational companies. Instead, it's written for hands-on leaders, for aspiring entrepreneurs, for busy managers, for small business owners, for nonprofit administrators, for project coordinators and for anyone else who wants to transform their important ideas into reality. Developing a strategy can be complicated, but it doesn't need to be. This book deconstructs the strategic planning process, stripping it down to its bare essence and removing all the business school jargon. Then it is reconstructed as a simple and clear five-step process that is useful for any type of strategy. This simple strategic planning process will help you clarify your vision and map out a concrete plan for achieving it.

Michael Beard
Simple Group Global
Hanoi, Vietnam

SECTION 1:
THE BIG PICTURE

Survey and test a prospective action before undertaking it. Before you proceed, step back and look at the big picture, lest you act rashly on raw impulse.

Epictetus

Though written nearly two thousand years ago, the stoic wisdom of Epictetus is still practical advice for today. So, let's step back and get a birds-eye view of strategy and the strategic planning process in the first part of the book before diving into the nitty-gritty details. In Chapter 1, we'll consider reasons why you might want to develop a strategy. Chapter 2 will explore an overview of the five basic steps in the strategic planning process to see how they fit together. Finally, Chapter 3 will reflect on two foundational ideas that add fuel to strategy: core beliefs and core passions. Let's get started.

CHAPTER ONE

Why Have a Strategy?

Building a business is all about doing something to be proud of, bringing tal-ented people together and creating something that's going to make a real dif-ference to other people's lives.

Richard Branson

Why is developing a strategy important? If you already know what to do and how to get it done, then why bother going through the effort of ham-mering out a strategic plan? For example, let's assume you run a café. The business concept isn't too complicated. You buy quality coffee at wholesale prices. You add value by brewing the coffee in an espresso machine. You have a decent location where customers can find you easily and you do a bit of advertising to let folks know where they can get a great cup of java. With luck, you can sell enough to cover your expenses and turn a profit. If you are profitable, why worry about having a strategic plan?

STRATEGY CLARIFIES WHAT'S IMPORTANT

Why run a café? Why is it that important to you? Is it just to make money or something else? Developing a strategy forces you to answer these and other important questions. As you work through them, you begin to clarify your core beliefs and core passions. And your core beliefs and passions help define the purpose of your café. You might discover through this process (for example) that you want to run a café because you are passionate about great coffee and you care about clean agricultural products and economic fairness for farmers.

STRATEGY SETS DIRECTION

Strategy involves much more than clarifying what is important to your organization or team. It also sets the direction. Before the advent of modern navigation systems, sailors would chart their course by the stars. They would follow a bright star above the horizon and constantly check their course against the host of constellations in the sky. A good strategy always has a bright, shining star above the horizon that you can use to chart the course of your team or organization. Having a clear sense of direction helps you know how to use your time, people and resources more effectively.

STRATEGY DEFINES THE VALUE PROPOSITION

At the core of any organization or team is a basic value proposition that identifies a problem that you are trying to solve for others. A restaurant solves the problem of hunger for busy people living in the city. A humanitarian aid organization solves the problem of hunger for people trying to survive on less than a dollar a day. Solving problems is at the heart of strategic planning. A good strategy clearly defines the problem you are trying to solve and lays out a plan for solving it.

STRATEGY CONNECTS THE PRESENT TO THE FUTURE

Strategy is like a road map that connects your current reality with your future reality. A well-crafted strategic plan undertakes a thorough analysis of your starting point. It considers all of your current resources and any factors presently influencing your organization or team. It also looks toward where you want to be in the future and then establishes a path to get you to that place. There are many ways to get from one place to another. But, at some point you need to choose one path. You can't travel down every possible road. This fact applies to strategy as well. You need to choose a path that best fits your organization or team.

STRATEGY GETS EVERYONE ON THE SAME PAGE

Imagine two groups of people working on two large jigsaw puzzles. Group A has decided to place the finished picture from the cover of the box at a prominent place on their table where everyone in the group can easily see it. They have also decided how they will go about putting the puzzle together, such as identifying all of the border and corner pieces and working on those first. Group B is a little less organized. One person hides the cover picture under the table where only he can see it. Another person decides to use a completely different picture as a reference. Still another person starts randomly grabbing pieces and trying to force them together. Now, let me ask you a question. Which group do you think will complete the puzzle first? It's obvious, isn't it? Since everyone in group A is working off of the same picture and has a plan for working together, they will likely leave group B in the dust.

This is what having a good strategy does for a team or organization. Everyone is on the same page looking at the same picture of the future. When everyone is on the same page, it's easier to work together. It's easier to decide what needs to be done and how to go about doing it.

STRATEGY TURNS BIG IDEAS INTO REALITY

Not everything in life needs to be part of a strategy. In most cases, you don't need a strategic plan for accomplishing life's routines like eating lunch, commuting to work and grocery shopping. Though a strategy might involve seemingly mundane tasks, the focus is on how those tasks help you turn a big idea into reality with a team of people. If routine activities are needed to bring a your idea to life, then those activities become part of the strategy. If not, don't worry about trying to make them strategic. Some examples of strategies might include: a plan for growing your business; a marketing plan for your company; or a social impact plan for your nonprofit.

Now that we know some of the reasons for developing a strategy, let's move forward and explore the basic steps in the strategic planning process.

CHAPTER TWO

Overview of Strategy

Leaders establish the vision for the future and set the strategy for getting there.

John P. Kotter

Have you ever had one of those toy metal construction sets? You know the kind. It comes in a box with various shapes and sizes of steel brackets, nuts and bolts like the one pictured in *Figure 1*.

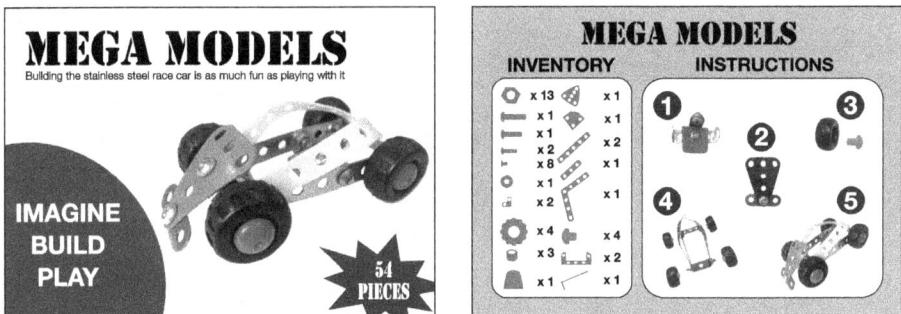

Figure 1: Construction Set

The box has a picture of an airplane or car on the front and a list of parts with a set of instructions on the back. If you have ever had one of these sets, then you already know the five basic steps of any strategy.

1. Observe the front of the box. It gives you a *picture of the future*, an image of the completed car.

2. Look at the back of the box to see an *inventory* of parts and tools that are inside the box.

3. The car is broken down into a few *major parts* (driver's seat, hood, wheels and frame).

4. There is also a *set of instructions* that show you how to assemble the individual pieces.

5. As you build you constantly *evaluate* your progress by comparing your creation with the picture on the front.

Putting all five steps together creates a strategy map (see *Figure 2*). We'll explore each step of the strategy map in detail in the following chapters. For now, let's look at each step briefly in order to see how they are connected.

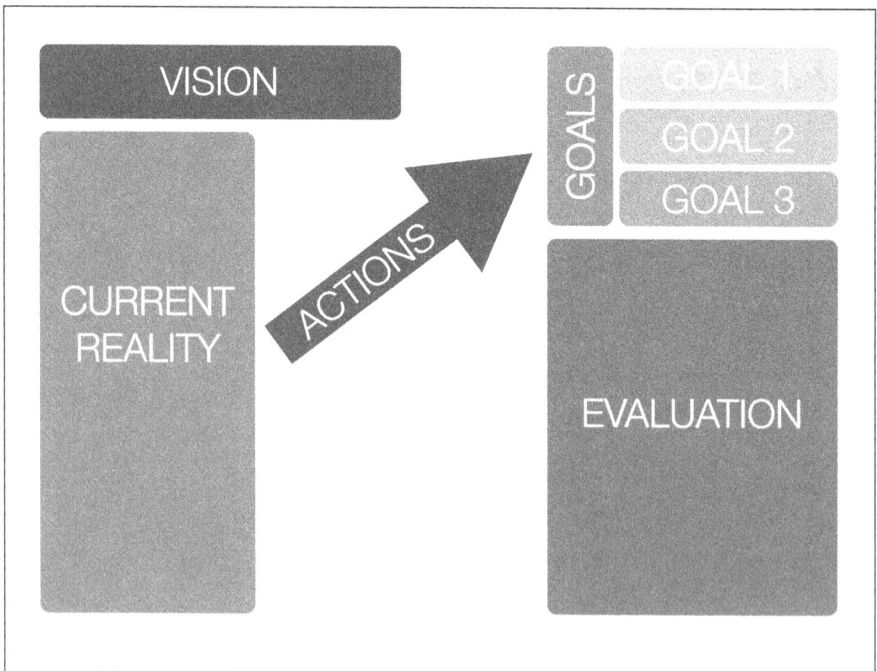

Figure 2: Strategy Map

STEP 1: VISION

Like a photo of a completed car on the front of the box, a good strategy be-gins with a clear picture of the future. There are actually two futures, the distant future and the near future. The distant future is perhaps 10, 20 or even 30 years down the road. This long-term picture is your *vision*. What do you want to achieve in 10, 20 or 30 years from now through your team or organization? Eradicate a preventable disease like malaria? Revolutionize the transportation industry? Create a new model of education? Colonize Mars? The near future is perhaps six months or one year from now. Once you have a clear picture of the distant future, you can translate that into a series of short-term goals that move you toward that vision of the future. These short-term goals will form the first part of the *instructions* for achiev-ing your vision (see step 3 below for further discussion about goals).

In Chapter 4, we will explore in more detail what goes into building a compelling vision. We will also see how an organizational vision relates to its mission and values. The terms *vision*, *mission* and *values* are so overused today that most people aren't sure what they mean and how they are related to each other. For most people, they are just something the marketing team thought up to post on the company website. We will demystify these three ideas and show you how to turn them into simple, clear and practical tools.

STEP 2: REALITY

Reality is your current situation and resources. This step is the process of taking inventory. It involves opening up your organization and dumping out all the parts and tools to see where you are and what you presently have to work with. When you take inventory of your organization, you get a clear picture of where to begin as you pursue your vision. It's a clear picture of your present reality. Chapter 5 will take a step back from your future vision to your present reality. It will introduce a simple tool to help you identity your current strengths, weaknesses, opportunities and threats. It will also explore five factors that influence your ability to pursue your vision.

STEP 3: GOALS

We all know people who dump out parts and just start building. They are convinced that they don't need to read the instructions. An hour later they finally consult the instructions. Then, ten minutes after that the model car is complete.

A good set of instructions is the critical component that connects your present reality to your future vision. It describes how you will get from here to there. The instructions in a strategic plan consist of two parts: a set of strategic goals (step 3) and an action plan (step 4) for achieving those goals.

As previously mentioned, goals are focused on the short-term future. Strategic goals break your vision down into a set of achievable objectives that can be accomplished over the course of a year (or less). Chapter 6 will show you how to look at your vision and your present reality in order to generate a list of potential goals. Most likely, you will end up with too many goals to pursue. Therefore, Chapter 7 will provide you with filters designed to help you sift through and identify the goals worth pursuing. Finally, Chapter 8 will guide you through the process of setting concrete goals and making them actionable.

STEP 4: ACTIONS

The second part of your set of instructions is a clear action plan that connects your current reality to your short-term future goals. It breaks your goals down further into a set of smaller tasks. Each task has people, time and resources assigned to it. It's like the specific instructions on the box that says things like, "Connect bracket A to bracket B with the 1 cm bolt and nut." Chapter 9 will survey all of the components of a practical action plan.

STEP 5: EVALUATION

As you are building a model car, you probably find yourself checking the picture and instructions often to see if you are putting the right pieces together in the right order. You also check to see how much you still need to build before the model is complete. This is the essence of the evaluation process.

The evaluation process is basically a set of specific measurements used to track the execution of a strategy. Chapter 10 will survey the evaluation process. It will explore three basic questions:

What will you measure?

How will you measure it?

How often will you measure it?

After investigating each step in a strategic plan, Chapter 11 will discuss the art of executing your strategy and Chapter 12 will consider the important role that collaboration plays in the development and execution of your strategy. That last chapter will bring it all together with some practice ideas for getting started.

In the next chapter we'll examine the role that beliefs and passions play as you develop a strategy. Core beliefs and core passions are the foundation on which strategies are built. They are not just components or steps of a strategy. Rather, they form the environment in which your strategy lives and breathes.

CHAPTER THREE

Core Beliefs and Passions

This age will die not as a result of some evil, but from a lack of passion.

Søren Kierkegaard

Belief and passion motivate you to develop and stick with your strategy. They are the forces that push you through the challenges you will face. They also serve as reservoirs of energy when you need to work on the mundane aspects of your strategy. So, let's take a moment to understand what beliefs and passions are and how they influence strategy.

Beliefs and passions are interconnected. The things that we believe are also the things we are passionate about. Our beliefs stir our passions, and our passions uncover what we truly believe. If you find that you are not passionate about something, then you probably don't believe in it. We see this all the time in relationships. If you believe that your family is important, you will be passionate about spending time with them. Likewise, if you are more passionate about spending all of your time at work instead of with your family, then you don't really believe that your family is important.

WHAT IS A BELIEF?

A belief isn't the same thing as *blind faith* (like believing in Santa Claus or the Tooth Fairy). True beliefs are rooted in our knowledge of and our truth about reality. But, a belief is something more than simply acknowledging a set of facts. Our beliefs move us beyond mere intellectual assent into action. When we truly believe something, it changes our behavior. Beliefs are essentially convictions that translate into actions.

On a cognitive level, you might accept the fact that a healthy diet and regular exercise will result in weight loss. But, that isn't the same as believing that *you* will lose weight by changing your diet and exercise routine. Perhaps what you really believe is that being overweight is in your genes or that you just don't have the willpower to eat healthy and exercise regularly. Psychologists use the term *limiting beliefs* to describe beliefs that prevent us of from taking the actions we *know* we should take.

Belief also demands trust. Danish philosopher Søren Kierkegaard refers to a *leap to faith*. He argues that trying to obtain absolute certainty about the big questions in life is a futile exercise. You might have good reason to assume the sun will come out tomorrow because it has every morning so far, but can we know this with absolute certainty? Perhaps all the scientists are wrong about the life expectancy of the sun. Perhaps it will implode tomorrow and destroy our entire solar system. After all, the medieval scientists were wrong about the earth being flat. Kierkegaard would say this kind of skepticism is useless and debilitating. At some point we just need to trust that the sun will come out tomorrow and live life as if it will. We need to step out and move forward in spite of any uncertainty. We need to take a *leap to faith*.

Wait a minute! This isn't a philosophy book. Why should I care about Danish philosophers and the nature of belief anyway? How does this fact relate to strategic planning? Well, strategy begins by looking at the future. Once we start imagining the future, we leave the realm of certainty and enter the territory of belief. Tomorrow offers no guarantees. The future is not certain. That's why you need to let go of certainty and hire belief as your guide. If you don't believe that your dream of the future can become a reality, then you won't take that leap to faith that is necessary to make it happen. Dr. Martin Luther King, Jr. said during his Noble Peace Prize acceptance speech, "faith can give us courage to face the uncertainties of the future."

EXERCISE:

Take a moment to think about something personal and specific that you would like to see happen in the future. Perhaps you would like to change careers or finally lose weight and lead a healthy lifestyle. As you contemplate that ideal future, you will probably notice that several limiting beliefs pop into your mind to keep you from making that leap to faith. Sayings like, "I can't lose weight because I am genetically predisposed to be overweight" or "I can't afford to change careers at this stage in my life." Now, write all those limiting beliefs down as they come to mind. Then challenge each of them. Say to yourself, "Am I really genetically predisposed to be overweight?" Most limiting beliefs are actually absurd when you stop to think about them. Find the absurdity in each limiting belief. Finally, rewrite each limiting belief into a positive belief. For example, "My genes don't determine my weight; my choices determine my weight."

SHARED BELIEFS

Religions are built around a set of shared spiritual and moral beliefs. But, religions are not the only organizations with shared beliefs. Schools form around a set of beliefs about how we ought to pass our knowledge onto the next generation. Unions form around a belief in the dignity of workers and their rights as citizens. The National Aeronautics and Space Administration (NASA) is formed around the belief that space exploration will move the human race forward. Hospitals are formed around a belief in the power of medicine to heal. The United States was founded on the belief that all men are created equal, that they are endowed by their Creator with certain unalienable, and among these rights are life, liberty and the pursuit of happiness (*Declaration of Independence*). What are some shared beliefs in your team or organization?

CORE BELIEFS

You can probably list a number of shared beliefs in your team or organization, but it is important at this stage to identify and clarify shared core beliefs. As we mentioned earlier, beliefs are convictions translated into actions. Strategy is all about identifying and engaging in actions that move your organization from your present reality to your vision of the future. Therefore, your core beliefs will have a massive influence on your strategy. Your core beliefs will heavily influence your vision.

The humanitarian aid organization Charity Water shares a core belief that clean drinking water has the power to improve health, improve education and improve opportunities. This core belief is boldly proclaimed on the home page of their website, "Clean Water Changes Everything." Everything that Charity Water does as an organization flows out of this core belief. It also shapes their vision of providing clean water access to everyone.

Tesla Motors embraces a core belief in sustainable energy. Their strategy reflects this core belief as they state, "Tesla's mission is to accelerate the world's transition to sustainable energy." Tesla Motors isn't satisfied with just making a great electric car (though they are leading the industry). Rather, they want to push forward the advent of sustainable transportation.

If you feel inspired after reading about Charity Water or Tesla Motors, there is a good reason. As humans, we connect with beliefs, not programs or products. Our natural response to programs and products is, "So what? Why should I care?" Why should I care that your biotech company makes innovative medical devices? Why should I care that your nonprofit provides microloans to people in a country I've never heard of? Why should I care about your political party's new tax plan? The fact is that people don't care about medical devices, microloans and tax plans. However, if your biotech company believes in the value of saving lives, it will resonate with medical professionals who also care about saving lives. If your nonprofit believes that poverty reduction is a moral obligation, then it will resonate with those who share that belief. If your political party believes in economic justice, then others who also champion economic justice might get behind your tax plan. When we communicate what we believe, we inspire people who share our beliefs to build a vision around those beliefs.

Belief is highly contagious. Communicating our beliefs can inspire others to start believing. Maybe you never thought much about clean water until you read about Charity Water's belief that clean water changes everything. As you think about the profoundness of that belief, it resonates with something deep inside. You think about what life would be like if you didn't have access to clean water. Then you buy in to that belief and find yourself wanting to make a donation toward the construction of water wells.

WHAT ARE PASSIONS?

Passions are not simply strong emotions. Emotions are often influenced by our circumstances. Someone burglarizes your home and you feel angry and violated. You win the lottery, so you feel excited. Emotions are an important part of being human. If your emotions fit the circumstances, they are healthy. It's normal to feel angry and violated when someone burglarizes your home. But, sometimes we lose control of our emotions. Road rage is an example of a misplaced emotion.

Our passions, however, do not come from our circumstances. Rather, they flow out of our beliefs and convictions. We are passionate about the things we believe regardless of the circumstances. Our passions don't ebb and flow with changing circumstances. Let's look at political passion as an example.

Let's say that you are passionate about your party's political platform (its beliefs). That passion isn't dependent on who's in office. You might feel depressed when your party loses a key race, but you are still just as passionate about your political beliefs in spite of the loss. In fact, losing an election might stir passions even more.

The only thing that can change your passions is a shift in your beliefs. When I was younger I thought I had the world of politics figured out. Most issues were black and white and I held some pretty dogmatic political views. As I've grown older some of my political beliefs have softened and others have shifted completely. As a result, my attitude has changed about some issues that I used to be very passionate about. Likewise, I am now passionate about other issues that I wasn't passionate about when I was younger.

Like beliefs, passions drive people to action. There are two types of runners in the world represented by my wife and myself. My wife is passionate about running. She loves the challenge of training for a marathon. She feels compelled to run often and misses it when circumstances keep her from running for several days in a row. She talks about chasing after the runners' high. Her passion for running flows from her belief that running is fun and that it a great way to keep fit. Then, there's me.

I am not at all passionate about running. Training for a marathon is a form of cruel and inhumane torture in my opinion. I have never in my life felt *compelled* to run. The whole runner's high thing is a mystery to me (though I have personally encountered the runners' low on several occasions). My lack of passion for running comes from my belief that running is a form of penance for drinking too much beer.

SHARED PASSIONS

People with similar passions form tribes. Every summer hundreds of thousands of full-grown adults dress up like superheroes and descend upon the streets of San Diego, California for the annual *Comic Con*. I happened to be visiting San Diego one summer during the convention. Strolling down the street, I felt very safe knowing that I was within earshot of a few hundred versions of Wolverine and Spiderman. As I waited for the crosswalk to turn green, the Batmobile and the Ghostbusters wagon whooshed by. No bad guys would dare attack with that many superheroes around. Comic Con has been extremely successful about tapping into people's passion for superheroes in order to form a massive tribe of people who are very happy to spend thousands of dollars to dress up in a Halloween costume for the weekend.

Why are people so passionate about superheroes anyway? Superhero mythology taps into several deeply held human beliefs. As humans, we believe in honor and justice. We believe that bad guys should not get away with doing bad things. We believe that vulnerable members of society need to be protected and defended. We believe that people need to stand up against evil. We believe that the world needs heroes who will stand up for what is right. And, deep down inside we all want to be that hero. Therefore, average people all over the country have a chance to enter the story and become a hero for a weekend at Comic Con.

Comic Con is just one example of an organization that has tapped into a powerful set of shared passions. What about your team or organization? What are your shared passions? If you can identify and tap into those shared passions, you will build a tribe that is extremely motivated to execute your strategy.

CORE PASSIONS

Great organizations are able to identify and harness a set of core passions that can be used to build and execute their strategic plans. People are not inspired by strategies and plans. Rather, they are inspired by the core beliefs and passions on which those strategies are built. If you have already identified your core beliefs, it will be easy to identify your core passion. For example, if your organization is formed around a core belief in social justice, then your people will be passionate about strategies that promote social justice.

RELATIONSHIP BETWEEN CORE BELIEFS AND PASSIONS

What is the difference between beliefs and passions and how are they connected? As mentioned earlier, a belief is a *conviction translated into action. Passion is the translator.* Passions are focused on finding and executing actions that bring our beliefs to life. At the beginning of this chapter, we explored family relationships. If you believe that your family is important, your passion for your family will drive you to spend time with them. I'm sure you've run into a grandfather who loves showing you pictures of his grandkids. That's another example of passion. He believes that his grandkids are amazing, so his passion drives him to brag about them.

Habitat for Humanity provides another example of the relationship between core beliefs and passions. On their website they explain, "At Habitat for Humanity, we build. We build because we believe that everyone, everywhere, should have a healthy, affordable place to call home." The people at Habitat are *passionate* about building homes. Building homes isn't just what they do. It is what they love to do. Why do they love to build homes? They love to build homes because they *believe* that everyone should have a healthy and affordable place to call *home*.

HERE ARE OTHER EXAMPLES OF ORGANIZATIONAL CORE BELIEFS AND PASSIONS.

The nonprofit organization known as Technology, Entertainment and Design (TED) *believes* in the power of ideas. They are *passionate* about spreading ideas through TED Talks, conferences and online videos.

The country of Bhutan *believes* that the happiness of its citizens is more important than economic development. They are more *passionate* about increasing Gross Domestic Happiness (GDH) than Gross Domestic Product (GDP).

Zappos.com *believes* that customer satisfaction is more important than selling shoes (though they are the Internet's largest online shoe store). They are *passionate* about making customers happy even if that doesn't involve selling shoes.

ONE Campaign *believes* that extreme poverty can be eradicated. Over eight million volunteers around the world are *passionate* about campaigning and advocating for policies that promote justice and equality so that they can *make poverty history*.

EXERCISE: PYRAMID CONVERSATION

Organize a three-step *Pyramid Conversation* with your team or the key leaders in your organization. This conversation can take place at one time or it can be broken up into three sessions. If you choose to have the entire conversation in one sitting, you will need to block out a couple of consecutive hours.

As a side-note, you can use this three-part *Pyramid Conversation* to discuss anything presented in this book with your team. Pyramid Conversations are a great way to make sure everyone on the team has the opportunity to be heard (even the quiet people). This tactic also prevents dominant personalities from hijacking conversations.

PART 1: INDIVIDUAL RESPONSE

We are talking about an individual's internal conversation. Each person thinks and writes down a response to a specific question(s). This can be done prior to the meeting by email or during the meeting. The important thing is to let each person ponder the question(s) and respond in writing as an individual.

For this exercise, ask team members to describe in broad terms your organization's primary industry or area of work. Is it a technology company, financial institution, school, crisis relief nonprofit? Next, make a list of three to five beliefs that you feel very strongly about as they relate to your organization's primary industry or area of work. Write each belief starting with the phrase, "I believe . . ." For example, "I believe schools should focus on learning, not grades."

PART 2: SMALL GROUPS

Next, organize small groups of three to five people. One at a time, each person will share his/her responses. Someone can write them on a flip chart or whiteboard. Then, the group should place similar beliefs together. For example, the following two beliefs could be grouped together: "I believe schools should focus on learning, not grades"; and, "I believe that teachers should show students how to obtain useful knowledge and skills, not pass tests." Shared beliefs will rise to the surface through this conversation.

Discuss and create a new consolidated list of three to five beliefs that most people in the group share. Perhaps there will be some beliefs that only one or two people feel strongly about. It is important to recognize and validate those beliefs. It is perfectly fine for individuals to feel strongly about some beliefs that are not felt as strongly by other group members, but the group should remember that their goal is to identify beliefs that are shared.

PART 3: WHOLE GROUP

Finally, choose a facilitator (preferably not the organizational or team leader) to guide the team through the discussion. Your objective is to generate an *Organizational Statement of Faith.* Many denominational churches use a *Statement of Faith* to identify their core beliefs that might distinguish them from other denominations. Look up a few church websites for examples. Obviously in this exercise you will not be crafting a theological statement (unless you are a religious organization).

Gather everyone in one big group. You will essentially repeat the same process you did in *Part 2.* However, this time each small group will share their consolidated list rather than individual responses. Again, write the beliefs on a flip chart or whiteboard and group similar beliefs. Discuss and identify three to five broadly shared beliefs. At this point, as a group, you can craft an *Organizational Statement of Faith,* or you can assign the task to a group member.

SECTION 2:
FIVE STEPS OF A STRATEGY

He came to understand that tearing things apart was a powerful aspect of human nature.

Patti Smith

Chapter two provided a general overview of the strategic planning process. Now it's time to deconstruct the process and consider each of the five steps more carefully. When we do this, you will see how each step works and how they are connected to the other steps. For the most part, the process is sequential. But, you will find as you work through each step that it might cause you to refine some or all of the previous steps. If this happens to you, don't worry. That's part of the process as well.

If you've never developed a strategic plan, doing so for the first time might require more time than expected. However, with practice, your team will become faster and more efficient at strategic planning.

CHAPTER FOUR

Step 1: Vision

If you are working on something exciting that you really care about, you don't have to be pushed. The vision pulls you.

Steve Jobs

Imagine that you've planned to take a three-day hike up a very large mountain. At the beginning, your goal--the summit--is a little too far off in the distance for comfort. Though it's a three-day hike away, that peak dominates the crystal clear skyline and compels you forward. A marked trail leads the way. All you need to do is follow that trail and keep your eye on the mountain. Well, that's not exactly all you need. It's a three-day hike, so you're going to need supplies like food, water, a tent and a sleeping bag for starters. Though your backpack is full, you have left a host of items behind. You didn't pack your big screen TV, food processor or last year's tax returns. You only packed what you need to get you to the top of that mountain.

Okay, so where am I going with this? Well, the mountain hike is a metaphor for the three essential ingredients in the first step of building a strategy: vision, mission and values. See Figure 3. I know what you're thinking: "not another book about writing the perfect mission statement." Let me set you at ease—that's not where I'm going in this chapter. If you really want a slick mission statement to hang on your office walls, then visit Comfy-Chair's online mission statement generator (*www.lotta.se/mission-state-ment-generator/*). They'll generate a great sounding (but totally useless) mission statement in seconds. Vision, mission and values are not about wordsmithing statements. Let's take a closer look.

Figure 3: Vision, Mission and Values

VISION: THE MOUNTAIN

Vision is Big, Bold, Clear

Like a majestic mountain peak rising from the horizon, a good vision is big and bold. Though it is far off in the distance, it is crystal clear every time you look up. On May 25, 1961, President John F. Kennedy shared such a vision for the US space program. In a speech before congress he announced, "I believe that this nation should commit itself to achieving the goal, before this decade is out, of landing a man on the moon and returning him safely to the Earth." Now that's a big, bold and clear vision.

After reaching the moon, NASA spent the next few decades on shuttle missions and exploring the galaxy with drone ships and high tech telescopes. The mission was clear (space exploration), but there wasn't a clear vision for after the moon landing. Then, one day, along comes this Silicon Valley tech Chief Executive Officer (CEO) Elon Musk. He had an idea for a new company called SpaceX that would make more powerful and efficient rockets. But Musk's vision was reminiscent of JFK's. Musk announced that SpaceX wants to colonize Mars in order to save the human race from extinction. Sounds like something right out of a Sci-Fi movie. However, Musk is dead serious and has already invested billions of his own dollars to make it a reality. Only time will tell, but there's no arguing that his vision is big, bold and clear.

Vision is Future Focused

Nobody climbs Mt. Everest in a day. If you are new to climbing, five to ten years of training might be required before you can even attempt Everest. A trained and experienced climber might make several attempts before successfully summiting the foreboding peak. Each attempt will require several weeks on the mountain just to acclimate to the altitude and the thin air. A true vision is the same. It's not something you can accomplish in a day, a week or even a year. It will demand your blood, sweat and tears for a long, long, long time. It might take five, ten or even twenty-five years.

Landing a man on the moon wasn't something that NASA would accomplish in a month. It would require most of the decade and hundreds of thousands of work hours. Planning and orchestrating would require the best scientific minds on the planet. It would require the creation of technology that didn't exist in 1961. It would require the most rigorous training that any military pilot had ever experienced. Likewise, we don't expect that Elon Musk will colonize Mars next week. In fact, one of SpaceX's first attempts at simply sending a payload rocket into orbit ended in a spectacular explosion on the launch pad disintegrating both the rocket and their customer's satellite.

Vision is Compelling

Another point about vision is that it's compelling. President Kennedy could have stood in front of the crowd that day and said, "The United States will become the strategic leader in the aerospace industry by developing state of the art technologies and engaging in cutting edge programs to further our scientific knowledge of the universe." That's a statement that would look great on the walls of NASA headquarters. But it's certainly not as compelling as "landing a man on the moon and returning him safely to the Earth."

Vision Sets the Direction

The peak of a big, bold mountain can be seen from miles away. It stands as a constant visual reminder of where you are going. It sets your direction. If you are trying to get to the peak, you keep it in your sight and take one step at a time toward it.

Have you ever wondered how farmers plow perfectly straight rows? A common technique involves fixing their eyes on a stationary reference marker like a tree on the other end of the field. Then they start moving directly toward the reference point. A vision is a reference point off in the distance that we keep our eyes fixed upon to keep moving toward.

It is important to know your reference point, to know where you are headed. Unfortunately, many organizations don't know where they are going. They just know that they are going somewhere. In *Alice's Adventures in Wonderland*, Lewis Carroll brilliantly illustrated this predicament in this short dialogue between Alice and the Cheshire Cat:

> *"Would you tell me, please, which way I ought to go from here?"*
> *"That depends a good deal on where you want to get to," said the Cat.*
> *"I don't much care where—" said Alice.*
> *"Then it doesn't matter which way you go," said the Cat.*

"—so long as I get somewhere," Alice added as an explanation.
"Oh, you're sure to do that," said the Cat, 'if you only walk long enough."

If you don't know where you are going, then any road will take you there. Like Alice, most organizations just want to "get somewhere." That is why vision is so important. Vision sets our direction. It tells us where we are going and which roads take us there. If a road isn't heading toward your vision, don't take it.

Vision Explains the WHY

Vision also answers the question, "Why?" Many organizations put the cart before the horse. They spend all their time talking about what they do. We make great computers. We deliver cutting edge business consulting. We provide humanitarian aid. In his bestselling book, *Start with Why*, Simon Sinek points out:

> *Every single company and organization on the planet knows WHAT they do. This is true no matter how big or small, no matter what industry. Everyone is easily able to describe the products or services a company sells or the job function they have within that system . . . Very few people or companies can clearly articulate WHY they do WHAT they do.*

President Kennedy's speech highlights this as well. He clarified why the United States should send a man to the moon by explaining, "Now it is time . . . for this nation to take a clearly leading role in space achievement, which in many ways may hold the key to our future on earth." He believed that sending a man to the moon was critical for a better future for life on earth. He was essentially saying that we needed to put a man on the moon (what) so that we could create a better future on earth (why).

A Vision, not a Vision Statement

Hopefully, you now have a better understanding of vision. Before we move on, let's also talk about what a vision is not. A vision is not a vision statement. As I mentioned at the beginning of this chapter, we are not concerned with crafting great sounding statements to post on the walls. A vision is a clear and compelling picture in your mind. A vision is not a document; it's something you see.

If fact, you might find it difficult to articulate your vision in words. If you do, don't worry. You don't need the perfect words. Seeing the vision is much more important than writing the vision. After all, the basic definition of *vision* is "the state of being able to see." If you write a well-crafted vision statement filled with lofty sounding business terms that you can't picture in your mind, then you have missed the point. You don't have a vision. You merely have words on a piece of paper. A clunky-sounding statement that is crystal clear and compelling is far better than a well-crafted statement that is cloudy and uninspiring.

VISION EXERCISE: I HAVE A DREAM

Writing down your vision can be a useful activity. That might sound like a contradiction to what I just said about written statements. It's not. Although a written vision statement isn't all that important, the *process* of writing a vision statement is very helpful. Working to capture the essence of your vision in words helps you sharpen your vision even if you don't end up with a polished statement that sounds great.

Here are some helpful tips as you attempt to write down your vision. First, avoid industry jargon and buzzwords. Buzzwords and jargon are neither visual nor compelling. It may sound great "to become the industry leader of cutting-edge innovations." But it's not an image you can see easily in your mind. What does an *industry leader* look like? Can you hold a *cutting-edge innovation* in your hand?

Second, create word pictures. Imagine that you are someone living in medieval times. One night you have a dream with a crystal clear vision of a modern-day military attack helicopter. How would you communicate that vision to your medieval friends in a way they could understand? You don't have a word for helicopter because helicopters won't be invented for another five hundred years. The best way to communicate that vision is to use word pictures (metaphors). Rudimentary wooden machines existed in the middle ages and legends of fire-breathing dragons were widely circulated. So, you might tell your friends about your vision of a time in the future when mechanized fire-breathing dragons controlled by men will be used to fight battles.

Third, write a one-paragraph, "I Have a Dream" speech. Martin Luther King, Jr.'s famous speech at the foot of the Lincoln statue in Washington D.C. was basically his vision of racial equality in the United States. In his speech he repeated the phrase, "I have a dream that one day . . ."

> *I have a dream that one day this nation will rise up and live out the true meaning of its creed: 'We hold these truths to be self-evident: that all men are created equal.'*

> *I have a dream that one day on the red hills of Georgia the sons of former slaves and the sons of former slave owners will be able to sit down together at the table of brotherhood.*

> *I have a dream that one day even the state of Mississippi, a state sweltering with the heat of injustice, sweltering with the heat of oppression, will be transformed into an oasis of freedom and justice.*

> *I have a dream that my four little children will one day live in a nation where they will not be judged by the color of their skin but by the content of their character.*

I have a dream that one day, down in Alabama, with its vicious racists, with its governor having his lips dripping with the words of interposition and nullification; one day right there in Alabama, little black boys and black girls will be able to join hands with little white boys and white girls as sisters and brothers.

Now it's your turn. Try to express your vision in a short I-have-a-dream paragraph. Start each sentence of the paragraph with the phrase; "I have a dream that one day . . ." Once you have it written down, deliver it as a short speech to your team or key leaders to see if others find the vision compelling.

MISSION: THE TRAIL

Vision and mission are often confused with each another. If vision is the mountain peak, mission is the trail. Mission describes the activity of going up the mountain. The English word *mission* comes from the old Latin word *missio,* which means "to send." It was used by the Jesuits to describe the activity of priests going out to establish schools and churches. Mission is focused on action. What are you doing? I'm hiking on this path (mission). Why are you hiking on that path? I'm hiking on this path so that I can get to the peak of that mountain (vision). Vision describes where you are going. Mission describes what you are doing to get to your destination. The two are always connected.

Multiple parties can have the exact same vision while having very different missions. Let's assume that three people have the vision of traveling from Los Angeles to New York. One person books a direct flight to get there as quickly as possible. Another drives across the country so that he can visit several other states along the way. A third person travels west around the globe over a three-month period of time so that she can see the world as she goes.

It is important to stress that your mission always supports your vision. Mission is action that moves you toward your vision. During WWII, the European Allied forces' vision was to liberate Europe from the Nazis. The mission was fighting a series of battles starting with the invasion of Normandy. SpaceX has the vision of colonizing Mars. Their mission is to develop the rocket technology that will get them there.

One way to see if your mission supports your vision is to write a statement that connects the two ideas with the simple conjunction *so*. Elon Musk might write, "We develop new rocket technology (mission) <u>*so*</u> we can colonize Mars someday (vision)." The Allied forces might have said, "We are invading Normandy (mission) *so* we can liberate Europe from the Nazis (vision)." If your mission doesn't support your vision, it will be very obvious when you try to create a *so-statement*. For example, "We are invading Normandy *so* we can create jobs in Asia." Or perhaps, "We are developing new rocket technology *so* we can cure cancer."

MISSION EXERCISE:
CREATE A MISSION-SO-VISION STATEMENT

Describe your mission. How is your mission connected to your vision? How will your mission help you get up the mountain? Once you get your ideas on paper, try to formulate them into a *mission-so-vision* sentence as I just described. Write your mission as a short description of what you do and the vision as the reason for doing it. Here are several examples:

We sell direct trade coffee so we can create a fair economy.

We produce organic products so everyone can eat safe food.

We create medical equipment so we can extend life.

VALUES: THE BACKPACK

As we turn our attention to values, we're not talking moral values. Your moral compass should never shift. We're not recommending the "it's okay to cheat your customers if it will get you to the top of the mountain faster" mindset. Instead, we are talking about organizational values. For example, simplicity might be a core value for your organization. Though you believe that simplicity is critical to achieving your vision and mission, there is nothing morally right or wrong about choosing between complexity and simplicity.

A hiker's backpack carries the essential supplies needed to successfully complete the hike. Though a harmonica might be nice to have in your backpack to help pass time at night, you can probably make the climb without it. However, if you don't have a climbing rope you might not make it to the summit successfully. Likewise, values are essential organizational attitudes and values encourage behaviors that are critical to accomplishing your vision. They create an organizational culture. If these values are not shared and embraced by everyone on the team, then you run the risk of not making it up the mountain.

Values act like a compass that points you in the right direction. Sometimes the clouds move in and the mountain peak is difficult to see. Sometimes you get lost in the woods on the way up. When this happens your values will keep you on the path. A strong set of values will keep your team moving in the right direction.

The 2016 hit film *Hidden Figures* told the story of the vital role that a team of female African-American mathematicians played in successfully launching astronaut John Glenn into orbit. This was during a time when many parts of the United States were racially segregated including NASA. Katherine G. Johnson (played by Taraji P. Henson) was one of the African-

American women selected to work on the trajectory calculations and back-up paths for John Glenn's launch. In the film, she is seen having to walk long-distances across the sprawling NASA property to use the segregated colored restroom. An important organizational value for NASA surfaced when her superior Al Harrison (played by Kevin Costner) confronts Johnson for spending too much time using the restroom. She explains in frustration that she has to "walk to Timbuktu" in the rain to use the colored restroom. Her superior Harrison then realizes that NASA needs to embrace an organizational value of racial unity if they want to successfully launch a man into space. After tearing down the colored restroom sign, Kevin Costner's character says, "There you have it. No more colored restrooms. No more white restrooms. Just plain old toilets. Go wherever you damn well please. Preferably closer to your desk. Here at NASA we all pee the same color." Now that's an organizational value.

VALUES EXERCISE:
WHAT'S IN YOUR BACKPACK?

Take a few minutes to answer the following questions about your team or organization. Then, plan a time to discuss these questions with your team. Describe the contents of your backpack. What are your core values? What organizational behaviors do you need to keep you on the right path, up to the top of the mountain?

CHAPTER FIVE

Step 2: Reality

Yes, leadership is about vision. But leadership is equally about creating a climate where the truth is heard and the brutal facts confronted.

Jim Collins

You may have a clear and compelling vision of where you are headed, but do you know where you are right now? If you want to achieve your vision, it is critical that you know exactly where you are presently. Think about it in terms of booking a flight. Let's say that you want to plan a trip to Bangkok. When you book a flight online you can't just identify your destination city, Bangkok. There are two other critical pieces of information you need, your departure city and your travel dates. This critical information will determine what travel options are available to you. There might be a cheap flight from Sydney to Bangkok in May, but it won't be very useful if you live in Los Angeles and want to travel in June.

CURRENT REALITY AND RESOURCES

The next step in building a strategy is to identify your current reality. Describe reality, as it exists today, not as you envision it in the future. This will help you find your starting point. You also need to take inventory of the current resources at your disposal, things like time, people, equipment, property and finances. This inventory will help you know what you can use right away to get started and what resources you might need in the future as you move toward your vision.

Good to Great author Jim Collins calls this process "confronting the brutal facts." As you identify your current situation and resources, the worst thing you can do is try to make things look better that they are. You need to paint a true picture of reality even if it's not a pretty picture. If you don't have any money, you need to confront that brutal fact. If you don't have the right skill mix on your team, you need to confront that brutal fact. If you don't have the equipment you need to get to the top of the mountain, you need to confront that brutal fact.

Though this may sound depressing and demotivating, it is actually the opposite. If you know that you have a serious life-threatening disease and that following your doctor's orders is your best chance at recovery, you will be very motived to do whatever it takes to get healthy. Seeing your current reality in all of its ugliness makes the vision of the future seem that much more appealing. This is exactly what Dr. Martin Luther King, Jr. did through his practice of non-resistance to evil. By submitting himself (and other civil rights workers) to unwarranted abuse by authorities, he shined a light on the extent and severity of injustice that many suffered under segregation laws. Once Americans were able to see how bad the problem really was, it made Dr. King's dream of racial equality all the more appealing.

INTERNAL AND EXTERNAL REALITIES

As you examine your current reality, you can start with two broad categories: internal realities and external realities. The internal realities are those inside your team or organization: people, finances, systems, assets, liabilities, capital and anything else relevant to your vision. The external realities are those outside your team or organization. *STEP* is a helpful acronym for remembering four key areas outside your organization that you might want to consider: **S**ocial, **T**echnological, **E**conomic and **P**olitical conditions.

STRENGTHS, WEAKNESSES, OPPORTUNITIES AND THREATS (SWOT)

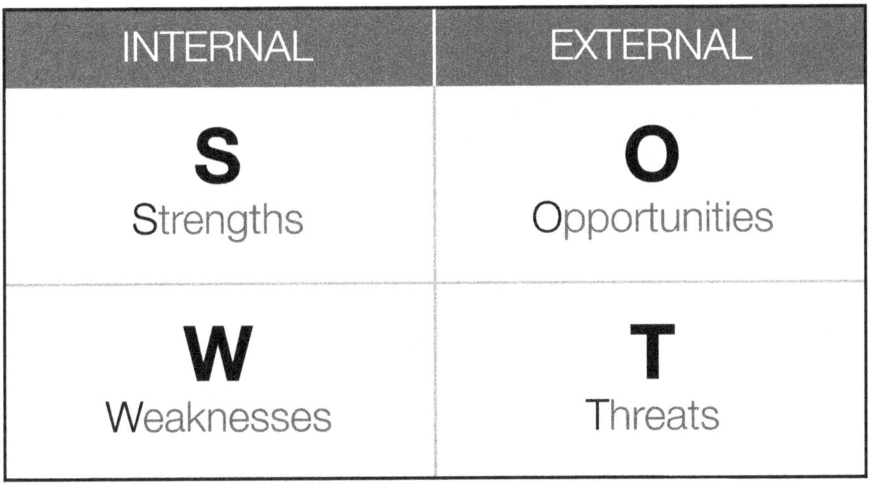

INTERNAL	EXTERNAL
S Strengths	**O** Opportunities
W Weaknesses	**T** Threats

Figure 4: SWOT Analysis

As you explore present internal and external realities, it's useful to categorize them as things that can help your vision and things that can hinder your vision. A SWOT analysis is a tool that does just that. SWOT is a simple acronym that stands for Strengths, Weaknesses, Opportunities and Threats (see Figure 4). Strengths are those realities inside your organization that can help move you toward your vision. Weaknesses are those internal realities that can hinder your ability to pursue your vision. Opportunities are external realities that (if pursued) have the potential of moving you toward your vision. Threats are external realities that could hinder you from pursuing your vision. Let's briefly look at each of these four categories of a SWOT analysis.

STRENGTHS

The first step in the SWOT analysis is to make a list of your internal strengths. What are your core competencies? What skill sets does your organization possess? What is your organization good at doing? For example, you might have a strong customer service system or a great design team. What internal resources do you have? Access to large amounts of capital? A great location? More than adequate facilities?

WEAKNESSES

Nobody enjoys looking at his or her weaknesses. But, this part of the SWOT analysis asks you to do that. It asks you to confront the brutal facts inside your team or organization. Maybe you have great customer service, but a poor marketing plan. Perhaps your team lacks critical skills that could seriously hinder your ability to move forward. Perhaps there are things that your organization is not good at that you should avoid all together?

You need to know your weaknesses for two reasons if you want to get up the mountain. First, if you don't know the breaking point of your climbing rope, you could get killed. Second, if you know that your current fitness level is inadequate for scaling a mountain, you can start a workout plan to increase your strength and stamina.

OPPORTUNITIES

As you look out on the external landscape, what opportunities do you see? Is a niche segment being served by no one? Do other teams or organizations out there share your vision? Could partnering with them benefit both of you? Could you acquire an asset that would improve your organization's efficiency? Are there technologies that could make your organization more productive? Are there government programs that could benefit your organization?

THREATS

Threats are factors that could potentially kill your vision or derail your team. They are the external brutal facts. For example, imagine that you operate an organic vegetable farm, but your neighbor has a habit of spraying harmful chemicals on his land. His spraying could contaminate your crop, invalidating your claim to be organic. Other questions to consider might be: Do you live in a politically unstable country? Are your suppliers' prices getting too high? Is there a new piece of essential technology that would make your current product irrelevant? Are there government regulations that could (if not followed properly) create legal problems?

FIVE FACTORS

Another tool that many businesses have found helpful for gaining an accurate view of their current competitive reality is *Porter's Five Forces*. Harvard Business Professor Michael E. Porter researched and analyzed five competitive forces that exert influence on all companies. He developed them into an analytical framework that many companies have used to build a competitive strategy in the marketplace. However, I believe that his framework has a broader application. Rather than limiting the scope to competition, I will apply his framework to any type of strategy. Therefore, I will refer to this framework as *five strategic factors* instead of *five competitive forces*. In some cases, I will also use different terms than Porter used in order to broaden the scope.

Factor 1: Setting

This factor describes the landscape in which your team or organization will operate. Again the STEP analysis (Social, Technological, Economic and Political) provides useful categories to consider, but there are other areas to consider beyond the STEP analysis. What impact could the physical environment (geography, climate, natural resources . . .) have on your vision? Are other organizations doing what you are doing? Are there opportunities to partner with them or are they competing with you for the same resources or clients? How many others are doing what you are doing? Is the landscape flooded with others doing what you are doing? If so, how are you differentiated (or how can you differentiate) yourself from them? Is there a segment not being serviced by others? Try to identify all aspects of the current environment that are relevant to your strategy.

Factor 2: Newcomers

Another factor to consider involves new entries in the current environment. How easy or difficult is it for newcomers to do what you are trying to do? If the investment is high or the process complicated, what are you doing to decrease the number of new entries. If there are newcomers on the horizon, who are they and what do they bring to the table? What impact (positive or negative) might these newcomers have on your strategy? Are there opportunities to partner with any of them, or will they compete with you for resources or clients? Are there segments of the landscape or segments of work that you can give to these new entries that will help you focus on the heart of your strategy. Compare your situation to that of a general contractor who employees sub-contractors. A general contractor wants to focus on the entire building. Sometimes he subcontracts work to specialists like electricians and plumbers so that he can focus on the larger task of building the house without getting distracted by the details of installing the electricity and plumbing.

Factor 3: Substitutions

The next factor focuses on potential substitutions. Let's assume your vision is to provide clean drinking water by digging sustainable wells. Are other organizations trying to provide clean drinking water from a completely different source such as rainwater collection or saltwater desalination plants?

Substitutions fulfill the same need, but from different angles. There are many ways to obtain clean water (wells, desalination, rainwater collection, sewage water reclamation, pipelines, etc.). That isn't necessarily a problem. The more ways we can make clean water accessible, the better. However, some substitutions can replace what you have to offer, making your strategy irrelevant. There are many examples of this fact in the business world. Napster (and later iTunes) replaced the local record shop. Netflix replaced Blockbuster. Amazon replaced the big chain bookstores. We also see examples outside of business. Text messages, Skype, and FaceTime have effectively replaced the Talk To You (TTY) service that the deaf and hard-of-hearing used to communicate with each other. In many developing countries, mobile phones and cell towers have replaced the need for the government to invest in landlines. There is also a push to replace fossil fuels with clean and renewable forms of energy like solar and wind.

Factor 4: Clients

Clients are the people you serve whether you represent a business or a non-profit. They can have a major influence on your strategy as well. Your strategy might involve offering specific services to clients, but what would happen to your strategy if your clients were simply not interested the services you are offering? Often you need to charge your clients for the goods and services you provide. How will they respond to the price you are charging? In the age of social media, clients can also help or harm your organizational reputation with the click of a mouse. And it is quite possible that clients can find a way to solve their own problems without your help.

Factor 5: Suppliers

Every team or organization needs supplies. They could be material supplies like coffee beans and cups if you run a café. Supplies can be digital such as an organizational website and accounting software. They can also be utilities such as electricity and Internet service. Many supplies are critical to the vision of your organization. Imagine trying to start up a café without coffee beans and cups. Imagine trying to run a medical clinic without medical equipment and medicine. Imagine trying to create a web-based educational community without Internet service or electricity. So, it's important to recognize the influence that suppliers have.

Suppliers influence the costs of the supplies you need. For example, let's say your team is launching a mobile community library. You are going to need a lot of books. However, the more expensive the books are the fewer you can afford to purchase. Suppliers also influence production quality and timing of the supplies you need. Even if you can afford the supplies you need, will they arrive on time? Will they work properly? The number of suppliers is also something to consider. How many suppliers exist? The fewer your suppliers, the greater they can influence things like quality, price and time.

EXERCISE:
BOATS AND ANCHORS / ISLANDS AND ICEBERGS

Set aside time with your team to complete a *SWOT analysis*. If possible, incorporate the *Five Factors* in your SWOT analysis. A fun way do a SWOT analysis is to turn it into a metaphor. Metaphors have the power to unlock the creative side of the brain. Ask your team to think about boats, anchors, islands and icebergs. *Boats* are your strengths, assets that move your organization forward. *Anchors* are your weaknesses, those things that drag you down or prevent you from moving forward. *Islands* are opportunities that might be worth your time to explore. *Icebergs* are threats you should avoid. If you want to get really creative, you can cut sticky notes in the shape of boats, anchors, islands and icebergs. Then, ask team members to write strengths, weaknesses, opportunities and threats on the sticky notes and post them on a flip-chart with a picture of an ocean scene.

NOW WHAT?

Many organizations find the process of collecting data about their present reality a fairly straightforward task once they have tools like the *SWOT Analysis* and *Five Factors*. But, as soon as they finish this task, they are faced with the question, "Now what?" It's rather depressing to confront your brutal facts and then just stop. The whole point of this exercise is not to see how bad things are and then wallow in despair.

Think of this process as remodeling your kitchen. Once you have a vision of your ideal kitchen, you need to look at your current kitchen. You need to measure the space you currently have and decide if it's large enough or if you need to add to the current space. You need to decide what you plan to keep the same, what you plan to repair and what you plan to replace. We need to be willing to do an honest evaluation of our present situation and resources so that we can move toward our vision. The next chapter will survey several ways to translate your SWOT analysis into potential strategic initiatives.

CHAPTER SIX

Step 3a: Goals - Seeking Goals

The thing about goals is that living without them is a lot more fun, in the short run. It seems to me, though, that the people who get things done, who lead, who grow and who make an impact . . . those people have goals.

Seth Godin

Having completed a SWOT analysis and considered the five factors, you should now have a fairly clear picture of the current reality of your team or organization. In this chapter, you will learn several ways to use a SWOT analysis to generate a list of strategic goals that might be worth pursuing. Once you have a list of potential goals, you will need to sift through them (Chapter 7) to identify the goal you should pursue. Finally, you will need to set concrete six-month or one-year goals that can move you closer to achieving your vision (Chapter 8).

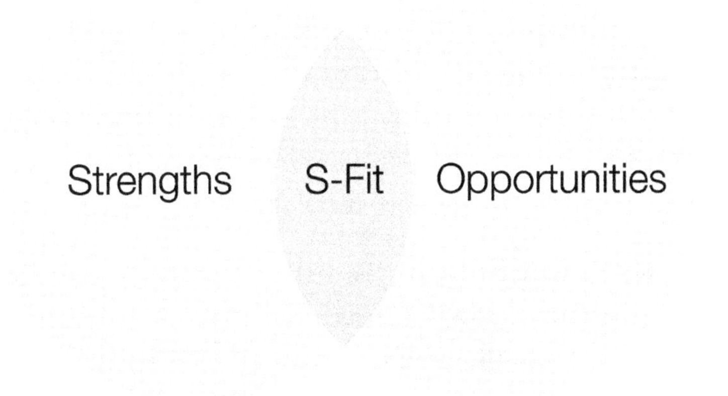

Strengths   S-Fit   Opportunities

Figure 5: S-Fit Strategic Goals

S-FIT GOALS

The "S" in S-Fit stands for "strengths." Take a look at your internal strengths and see if they overlap any external opportunities as illustrated in Figure 5.

For example, perhaps your company has developed a product line of affordable and healthy food products. From your SWOT analysis, you also discovered that there is a neighborhood close to your factory that has only fast-food establishments and convenience stores nearby. People living there have to drive about 20 minutes to get to an upscale health food store. The opportunity is a perfect fit for your core competency of making affordable, healthy food products.

OPEN SPACE GOALS

As you consider the Five Factors, look for Open Spaces that are not crowded with others who are trying to do the same thing. Marketing researchers, W. Chan Kim and Renée Mauborgne have coined the term Blue Oceans to describe these types of open spaces. They highlight the futility of entering into crowded market segments where competition is fierce. Instead, they suggest looking for market segments that are underserved or even non-existent. Based on the strengths you identified in your SWOT analysis, are you able to do something that few people are doing? Or perhaps no one is engaged. Can you deliver a product or service so far above industry standards that competition is irrelevant? Can you introduce something into the market that replaces current products with something different and better? This is what Netflix did to the video rental industry.

Nonprofits have Open Spaces as well. In 1986 the Carter Center was looking for ways to improve the health conditions of people living in underdeveloped communities around the world. Rather than focusing their efforts on issues like malnutrition and malaria prevention, they decided to focus on eradicating Guinea worm, an extremely painful and debilitating parasitic infection that incapacitates people for extended periods of time. However, nobody at the time was focused on preventing Guinea worm infections. It was an Open Space in the arena of preventable global health issues. So, the Carter Center launched its Guinea worm eradication initiative. In 1986 about 3.5 million people in Asia and Africa were suffering from this parasite. According to 2016 reports, there are now less than 25 cases globally. That's a 99.99% reduction.

DEVELOPMENT GOALS

Review the weaknesses listed on your SWOT analysis and identify areas that can be improved with a bit of focus and effort as illustrated in Figure 6.

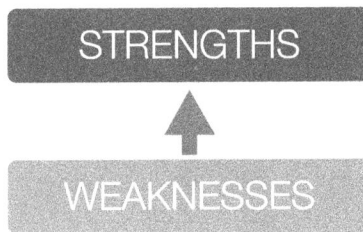

Figure 6: Development Goals

Do any weaknesses have a high potential of becoming strengths? For example, let's say you listed poor customer service as a weakness in your organization. Could it be improved by having your staff attend customer service training? Perhaps your nonprofit has a poor fundraising track record. Could this be improved by hiring a professional fundraiser?

HIDDEN OPPORTUNITY INITIATIVES

Next, take a look at the threats listed on your SWOT analysis. Sometimes opportunities are disguised as threats. Competition is often perceived as a threat in the business world. This thinking frequently leads to a brutal warlike strategy of trying to crush the competition. Most people assume that large competitors like Apple and Microsoft are out to destroy each other in a dog-eat-dog tech world. In 1997, Apple was on the brink of bankruptcy. They desperately needed an infusion of $150 million to keep from closing shop. Guess who came to the rescue? It was none other than the CEO of Microsoft, Bill Gates. Microsoft invested $150 million in Apple to keep them from failing. Why? Unknown to the public, Apple and Microsoft were teaming up to develop a number of strategic initiatives. One major project was the popular Microsoft Office Suite for Macs. This project was a strategic opportunity for both companies. Microsoft was able to sell its software to Mac users and more people were willing to buy Macs knowing that they could run MS Office.

RISK MANAGEMENT GOALS

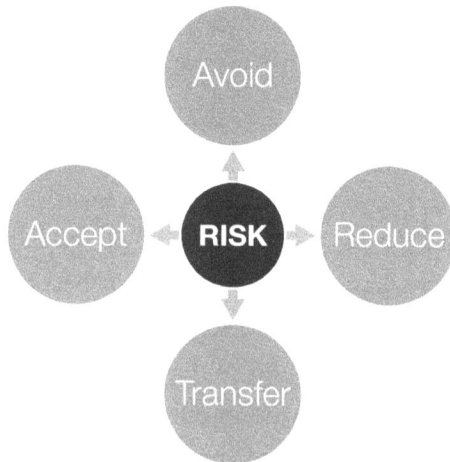

Figure 7: Risk Management Goals

Not all threats are hidden opportunities. Some threats are . . . well . . . threats. Perhaps you operate a mountain resort in an area that is prone to seasonal wildfires. The threat of a wild fire completely destroying your resort is a real risk factor. It would be difficult to find a hidden opportunity in a wild fire destroying your resort. Figure 7 highlights four options to consider as you seek to manage risks: avoid, reduce, transfer or accept.

For example, you might decide to avoid the risk of a wildfire destroying your resort by selling the property and reinvesting in a less risky location. A second option would be to reduce the risk by retrofitting the property with sprinkler systems and making sure that dry brush is cleared from the resort's surrounding area. A third option would be to transfer the risk to an insurance agency. You would pay a premium for fire insurance. In the event that your property is damaged or destroyed by a wild fire, the insurance company would pay for the reconstruction costs. Finally, you might determine that you have already taken all possible precautions and you accept the risk as part of doing business.

EXERCISE:

Follow the instructions below to generate several lists of potential strategic goals that might be worth developing into six-month or one-year goals.

1. **S-FIT:** List opportunities that align with your strengths or core competencies.

2. **Open Spaces:** List opportunities that are underserved or not being served by others.

3. **Development:** List internal weaknesses that can be improved by focused effort and potentially turned into a future internal strength.

4. **Hidden Opportunities:** Take a look at your potential threats. List threats that might contain hidden opportunities.

5. **Risk Management:** List threats that can be minimized or avoided with focused effort.

There are other useful models for generating potential strategic initiatives that won't be explored in this book, but I can mention two models that have gained large followings in the business world. One is known as the Balance Score Card developed by Robert S. Kaplan and David P. Norton. They suggest setting goals in four key areas: financial results; client satisfaction; internal organizational processes; and organizational learning and growth. Another popular approach among product manufacturers is known as Six Sigma. This model was developed by Bill Smith at Motorola in 1986 and became a central strategic framework for General Electric under CEO Jack Welch's leadership. The Six Sigma seeks to establish goals aimed at continually improving the manufacturing process. Many people have found practical applications of this model outside of manufacturing. If either of these models sounds useful, then please explore them further to generate even more potential strategic goals to consider. Once you have generated a list, the next chapter will provide filters for identifying which goals are worth pursuing.

CHAPTER SEVEN

Step 3b: Goals - Sifting Goals

Probably, indeed, the larger part of the labor of an author composing his work is critical labor; the labor of sifting, combining, constructing, expunging, correcting, testing. This frightful toil is as much critical as creative.

T.S. Eliot

Have you ever been to an ice-cream shop where there are literally dozens of delicious flavors to choose from? You stand there paralyzed by the choices staring at you through the glass case. You wrestle over which of the thirty plus flavors will make the cut and end up on your triple-scoop cone. Almond mocha fudge, peanut-butter chocolate or chocolate chip? Having too many choices (especially good choices) can be debilitating and hinder you from moving forward.

At this point in the strategic planning process, you have generated a list of potential goals that your team could pursue. Most likely, the list has too many goals to realistically pursue in the next six months to one year. If so, that's a perfectly normal conclusion of any type of brainstorming session. However, you need to move forward in the process of narrowing the list to a smaller and more realistic set of goals to actually pursue. Applying some filters can help.

Filters sift things out. If you want clean drinking water from a river, you need to filter out all of the potentially harmful stuff swimming around in the water. First, you need some coarse filters that remove the big things like leaves and dirt. Then, you need a set of fine filters that remove smaller particles and disinfect the water. The concept of coarse and fine filters is a practical analogy for the types of strategic filters you can apply to sift through potential goals. I'll present seven filters that you can use to determine if a particular initiative is worth pursuing. To make them easy to remember, they all begin with the letter "r."

COARSE FILTERS

Just as you would want to remove leaves and dirt from your drinking water, you might also want to remove from your strategic plan some potential goals that simply don't belong. The following three filters identify initiatives that might not fit your team or organization. You should say "no" to these initiatives, no matter how attractive they might look on the surface. Pursuing them will only distract you from your vision and drain your resources. Let's look at each filter separately.

Relevance Filter

The Relevance Filter assumes you have a clear vision and mission. This filter asks two questions: (1) Will this goal help us accomplish our vision and mission? (2) Will this goal distract us from our vision and mission? Some initiatives may seem attractive at first, but if they don't move you toward your vision, why bother? For example, consider an organization dedicated to eradicating HIV. Now imagine that the organization has an opportunity to develop a school nutrition program (a worthy cause no doubt). Perhaps they even have the internal skill sets and resources to develop a great program. The problem is obvious. Nutrition programs are simply not the vision or mission of the organization. This opportunity would ultimately distract the organization and steer valuable resources away from its main vision.

Reconciliation Filter

Does the initiative align with or violate your core values? Let's assume that you manufacture healthy beverages. One of your company's core values is producing healthy products. Your product development team is the best in the business. They consistently create great tasting, affordable beverages that do well in the marketplace. So, you are presented with an opportunity to make a lot of money by developing an inexpensive sugary fruit drink. Since your company is good at making inexpensive beverages that do well in the marketplace, this seems like a strategic fit. Although your company could make a lot of money from the initiative, you should say "no" because it violates one of your core values. Beverages high in sugar contribute to diseases such as diabetes. Producing such a drink would damage your brand and confuse your identity as an organization committed to making healthy products.

Risk Filter

Before developing strategic goals, your team should establish a risk ceiling. This is the maximum amount of risk you are willing to take with your time, finances, people and other valuable resources. What are you willing to lose by pursing the goal and what are you not willing to lose? If a goal presents a risk that exceeds your risk ceiling, then avoid it. A classic example is the 2008 financial crisis. Large banks like Lehman Brothers started taking reckless and excessive financial risks with subprime mortgages in order to expand their global financial impact. Their decisions resulted in a global financial crisis that the world hadn't seen since the Great Depression. Massive government bailouts and other measures were enacted to prevent a global economic collapse. When the dust settled, Lehman Brothers made the largest bankruptcy filing in U.S. history. Ultimately, the corporation had to liquidate its assets and sell off its operations.

FINE FILTERS

Now let's look at our Fine Filters. Just because an initiative makes it through the Coarse Filters doesn't automatically mean you should pursue it. "No" is only half of the answer. You need a bit more sifting to find the initiatives to which you can say "yes." The next five filters will help you in that process.

Return on Investment (ROI) Filter

The ROI filter asks if the initiative is worth the effort. Take a look at the ROI grid in Figure 8.

		LOW	MEDIUM	HIGH
R E T U R N	HIGH	Quick Wins!	Pursue	Consider
	MEDIUM	Consider	Consider	Probably not worth it
	LOW	Why bother!	Avoid	Avoid

INVESTMENT
(*time, money, focus, energy, resources, HR...*)

Figure 8: Return on Investment (ROI) Grid

The x-axis considers the amount of investment (people, money, time, etc.) the initiative requires. Investment can be high, medium or low. The y-axis considers the potential returns on the investment. These might include: financial gain, community impact, expanded customer base or a host of other things. The potential returns are also categorized as high, medium or low.

To the best of your ability, plot where a specific goal might be on the ROI grid. If the return is high and the investment is low, then you have identified a Quick Win. These are no-brainers. They are definitely worth pursuing because it won't require much effort, but will yield big results and will be very motivating to the team. Unfortunately, there probably won't be many initiatives that fall into this section of the grid. If the investment falls in the medium category, but the potential return is still high, then in most cases it would still be worth pursuing. However, if the investment is high and the potential return is high, you should rely on some of the other filters to help you decide.

Another no-brainer consists of goals that require a high investment, but would yield low returns. These are definite no's that you should avoid. Actually, anything that provides a low return is rarely worth pursuing. These types of goals end up being resource drainers. They also distract your people from pursuing more effective initiatives. Even if the investment is low for a low-return goal, the question still remains, Why bother? It's not much effort, but there's also not much return.

The maybe areas are where either the investment is medium or the potential returns are medium. They are labeled consider because that are not clearly yes or no options. They might be worth pursuing, but will require more discussion. Applying some of the other filters could provide additional clarity.

Resource Filter

When my four children were small, we often wanted to take them out to see a movie. However, for the price of the tickets, popcorn and drinks we could have purchased a small home (I'm exaggerating only a little). So, we had to weigh our desire to go to the movies with our available financial resources. Even though it would have been a fun family-centered activity, the required financial resources were often a stretch for us. Instead, we usually opted to rent a DVD and make popcorn in the microwave.

In one sense, this fine filter takes a closer look at the x-axis (investment) of the ROI grid and the Risk filter. It requires you to assess your available resources. Do you currently have enough resources (time, money, people, energy, etc.) to accomplish the goal? If not, how difficult would it be to acquire the needed resources? If you direct your resources toward accomplishing this goal, will it prevent you from pursuing more important goals? Perhaps, the resources are not beyond your risk ceiling, but are high enough to feel challenging. Therefore, an honest evaluation of your resources is required.

Right-Time Filter

Back in 1997, Chase Norlin launched a revolutionary website that allowed users to publically upload videos for anyone on the Internet to enjoy. The web technology was cutting edge. Users could upload almost any video file format to the site. No, Chase Norlin isn't the founder of YouTube. Though his website was very similar to YouTube, it predated YouTube by almost a decade. Norlin's innovative site was ShareYourWorld.com. However, you've probably never heard of ShareYourWorld.com.

Unlike YouTube, ShareYourWorld.com suffered major financial problems and eventually shut down in 2001. Four years later YouTube launched and became one of the most successful sites in Internet history. Why? What happened? The simple answer is timing. ShareYourWorld.com was a great idea that was well executed, but the Internet was simply too young and too slow. The Achilles heel of this platform according to Norlin was timing and Internet bandwidth. ShareYourWorld.com launched in the age of dial-up modems' painfully slow connection speeds. Uploading and streaming videos was too slow. It simply wasn't the right time to launch a video-sharing site.

Chase Norlin's story serves as an example of the Right-time Filter. As you sift through your goals, you need to determine if the timing for a particular initiative is ripe. Is it too early to work on a particular goal? Can you wait? What are the consequences of waiting? Would you miss a worthwhile opportunity by waiting for a greater chance of success?

Resolve Filter

Though some goals check all the boxes, you still need to ask if you have the support of your team or organization. You need to ask if there is enough resolve to pursue the goal. This is especially important if the goal is demanding of your time, people and other resources. Will your people get behind the initiative? If not, can you motivate them to get behind the initiative? It might be a great idea, but if your people are not supportive, it will never get off the ground. You need to ask if there is a critical mass of people committed to a particular initiative. You might have a great canoe and state-of-the-art oars, but if your team doesn't like the idea of rowing, you might reconsider entering the water.

After sifting through all the potential goals, you will end up with a new set of goals. At this point you might notice that some (or even all of your goals) are a bit vague. For example, you might determine that your company wants to improve its customer service. So, you write the goal, "We will improve our customer service this year." As you meditate on this goal, a number of questions might come to mind. What does improving mean? How much should we improve? What would it look like if we improved our customer service? What specific areas of customer service do we need to improve? How will we know if we are improving? The next chapter will present several ways to construct goals that are concrete and actionable.

CHAPTER EIGHT

Step 3c: Goals - Setting Goals

If something is important enough, even if the odds are against you, you should still do it.

Elon Musk

New Year's resolutions have a tendency to start off strong only to fizzle and die before the end of the first quarter. Perhaps part of the problem is that we make resolutions just because that's what you are supposed to do at the start of a new year. It's common to take a similar approach when it comes to setting goals in the professional realm. We set professional goals because . . . well . . . because it's professional to set goals. We hear the words of business gurus like Zig Ziglar ringing in our ears: "If you aim at nothing, you'll hit it every time." So, we aim at something, anything . . . it doesn't really matter what. As long as we are aiming at something, we just might get lucky and hit something, but we need to ask ourselves: "Why am I aiming at THAT target?" Not knowing why a goal has been set is often the reason for not achieving it.

MOTIVATION AND GOALS

If there is no internal, driving motivation to achieve your goals, you probably won't achieve them. When I was in high school, I was never very motivated to learn about basic car repair and maintenance. I assumed that I would pay a mechanic to take care of all that. This plan lasted until I had to pay for my first repair job. The mechanic's bill served as an incredibly motivating factor for me to set the goal of learning how to do basic repairs and maintenance. I quickly learned how to change the oil, repair a flat and replace the battery. I even tackled more challenging jobs such as replacing the brakes, changing the clutch and rebuilding the carburetor. I achieved all of these learning goals because I clearly understood and was motivated by the reason behind these goals: saving money.

Connect Goals to Vision

One way to tap into your internal motivation is to connect it to the clear and compelling vision. This is why having a compelling vision is so important. It lights a fire under our goals. Vision is the carrot at the end of the stick that inspires the horse to keep walking. Parents intuitively use this method to get their kids to eat vegetables. "If you finish your veggies, you can have an ice cream sundae," they promise. Their hope is that the vision of chocolate-covered bliss will sufficiently motivate the kids to finish off a serving of steamed broccoli. However, this method only works if the child genuinely sees an ice cream sundae as a desired reward. The same is true about vision. If you don't find the vision rewarding, then you won't care about achieving it. In turn you will not be motivated to accomplish the goals that move you toward that vision.

Break it Down!

Goals and vision are not the same although they are related. As previously discussed, a vision is something big and far off in the distance. Goals are much closer. Usually, they can be accomplished in six months to a year. They are essentially bite-sized chunks of your larger vision. Preparing to climb Everest might take ten years. You will need to be in excellent shape, so you'll need to set a fitness goal to physically prepare for the climb. You will need some intense climbing skills, so you'll need to set a training goal to increase your skill level. You're going to need professional gear, so you'll need to set a goal of selecting and purchasing the right equipment for the climb. The expedition will cost a lot of money, so you'll need to set a savings goal to cover your expenses.

Moving Forward, Not Checking Boxes

Many of us identify goals with making tick marks on a to-do list. Some of us find a lot of pleasure in checking off those little boxes on our lists. The point of setting a goal, however, is to move one step toward achieving a compelling vision. It's not about the little boxes. It's about progress, moving forward, making headway. It's about getting closer to the peak of the mountain. If you're the kind of person who finds pleasure in checking off boxes, that's great. Just don't stop there. Train yourself to see each of those little boxes as steps toward the mountain peak.

Connect Goals with Beliefs and Passions

In Chapter 3, we investigated how our beliefs and passions are interconnected. We also saw how our beliefs and passions inspire us to action. If you recall, our passions are not based on our current circumstances. They are rooted in deeply held beliefs. If you can recognize that your goals are actually a set of actions connected to your beliefs, you will become passionate about completing them.

What You Really, Really Want

The Spice Girls once sang, "Tell me what you want, what you really, really want." As it turns out, this is great advice for finding a goal that you are motivated to accomplish. You can start by asking, "What could I do to move toward my vision?" In Chapter 6 I suggested an approach for generating a number of viable options. However, now you need to ask, "What do I really, really want to do?" This question weighs all the potential goals against your motivation. If it's not something you really, really want to do then you probably won't do it. What you really, really want to do is likely something that you will find a way to do, no matter what challenges come your way.

SMAART GOALS

Yes, I meant to spell it with two letter A's. I added an extra letter to that acronym giving us SMAART goals. SMAART stands for: Specific, Measurable, Ambitious, Attainable, Relevant, and Timely. Let's briefly consider each of these aspects of a concrete and actionable goal. Once you have completed the process of filtering your goals and have identified the ones you are motivated to pursue, it's time to develop them into actionable objectives. Vague goals are difficult to pursue. If you are not really clear about what you are pursuing, you will find it difficult to know when you have achieved it. For example, let's assume that you decide to pursue a development goal about customer service. You know that your current customer experience is very poor. However, you are convinced that with a bit of focus, customer service could become a strength in your organization. Consequently, you set the goal: "We will improve our customer service this year."

At first glance the goal seems clear enough. However, it will quickly become cloudy as you start working on it. How will you begin the process of improving customer service? How will you know if you have improved customer service next year? What would great customer service look like? What aspect of the customer experience is in most need of improvement? You can add clarity to any of your goals by making them SMAART

You may have heard of the concept of developing SMART goals as a method of making your goals more concrete and actionable.

Specific

One way to improve a vague goal is to make it as specific as possible. Let's try this with that goal, "To improve customer service." We'll try to make this goal more specific by asking the following question: "What would improved customer service look like in our company?" Is there a specific aspect of customer service that most needs improvement? Maybe the refund policy needs to be made more customer-friendly. Perhaps employees could benefit from customer service training. Identifying the specifics of your goal will make it more concrete and actionable. For example, consider changing the goal to something more specific like, "We will create a customer-friendly refund policy" or "We will provide a customer service training program for our staff."

Measurable

Beyond making your goal as specific as possible, it is also helpful to know when you have completed your goal. Therefore, you need some ways to measure your goal. Let's say you have focused your goal on having your employees participate in customer service training so that you can improve the customer experience in your company. You might want to decide how much training they should do. Will they attend a series of training sessions throughout the year? If so, how many? You might also want to consider how you could measure the impact of that training on the customer experience. Perhaps your goal could include conducting a customer survey before and after the training.

Ambitious

Goals often require about six months to a year to complete. If a goal can be accomplished in a few days or a few weeks, then it really isn't a goal (at least in the context of the strategic planning process). If something can be completed in a few days or week, then it is a task, not a goal. The next chapter will explore tasks in greater detail. As you develop a goal, make sure that it is ambitious enough, something that will stretch your team or organization. Considering the customer service goal, it might not be ambitious enough to have your staff attend a one-hour customer service workshop. This goal wouldn't take much effort to achieve. It might require a few hours to organize and one hour of actual training. Though it will probably help the staff to some extent, you could probably do a lot more over the course of the year to improve customer service.

Attainable

Sometimes in a desire to make goals ambitious, teams can set goals that are too ambitious. They end up with goals that can't possibly be reached in a year's time. Becoming the largest global manufacturer of electric cars is a very specific and ambitious goal. However, it might be a bit too ambitious to achieve in one year, especially if you are a young start-up with only twenty employees. The goal is not impossible. Some companies like Tesla are well on their way of achieving this goal. It's just not achievable in a year's time. Therefore, as you attempt to make your goals ambitious, make sure that they are possible to achieve. Big visions inspire people because you have 5, 10 or even 20 years to pursue them. But, goals that are too ambitious to achieve in a year's time can have the opposite effect and create unnecessary frustration.

Relevant

One of the filters in the sifting process was to determine if your goal is relevant to your vision. If you have done a good job of filtering, you probably have a goal that is relevant. But, this is a good opportunity to double-check. Ask yourself, "How does this goal move us toward our overall vision?"

Timely

Goals are short term. You should be able to accomplish most goals over the course of a few months or as much as a year. There's no magic number for the amount of time a goal should take. It really depends on how much time is reasonable. For example, you might set a six-month target for training all of your employees in customer service whereas your sales goal might take a year to achieve. The key is finding a reasonable amount of time to set as a target. Give your team enough time, but not too much time. If you don't have adequate time to complete the goal, it creates stress and is very demotivating. However, allotting too much time creates inefficiencies. You might end up demotivating your people through boredom.

EXERCISE:

Make Your Goals SMAART. For each strategic goal, use the questions below to turn them into SMAART strategic goals.

Make it Specific

What is the specific outcome you want to accomplish?

What will it look like when this goal has been accomplished?

Make it Measurable

How will you know when you've reached this goal?

How can you measure your progress toward this goal?

Make it Ambitious

Is this goal too small?

Does the goal need to be bigger to stretch and challenge you?

Make it Attainable

Is this goal too big?

Can you accomplish it in less that a year or six months?

Do you have the resources to accomplish it?

Make it Relevant

How does this goal support your vision and mission?

How does this goal align your core values?

Make it Timely

By when will this goal be completed?

How long will it take to achieve this goal?

Final Version

Rewrite each goal as a SMAART Goal.

CHAPTER NINE

Step 4: Actions

Our goals can only be reached through a vehicle of a plan, in which we must fervently believe, and upon which we must vigorously act. There is no other route to success.

Pablo Picasso

Have you ever planned a long road trip? Many years ago, my wife and I planned to drive from Los Angeles to Washington D.C. Our goal was crystal clear: depart LA on Monday and arrive in DC by Friday. But, we didn't just jump in the car Monday morning and start driving. We divided our trip into a day-by-day plan. Before we left, we had the oil changed and our tires checked. We made sure we had a good spare tire and a roadside service contract in case the car broke down. We calculated how long we needed to drive each day to arrive in DC by Friday. We mapped out our driving route. We chose which interstate highways to travel and where to stop each night. Some nights we booked rooms at a motel and other nights we planned to stay with family and friends along our route. We even managed to plan sightseeing excursions along the way. In other words, we had a detailed plan to get us from LA to Washington D.C. in a week.

ELEMENTS OF AN ACTION PLAN

Planning a road trip is essentially the process of translating a strategic goal into a strategic action plan. Your goals are the destinations you want to arrive at in the next six months to a year. The big question now is, "How do you get from here to there?" Just like a road trip, you need a step-by-step set of instructions that spell out exactly how you will accomplish your goal.

This set of instructions is called an action plan. There are five elements to a solid action plan as illustrated in Figure 9: major steps, activities and tasks, resources needed; person(s) responsible; and deadlines.

Major Step:			
Activity / Task	**Person(s) Responsible**	**Deadline**	**Resources Needed**

Figure 9: Elements of an Action Plan

MAJOR STEPS

Start by breaking down the strategic goal into major steps. Each step is a "chunk" of related activities and tasks that move you toward your goal. For example, let's say your strategic goal is to develop a new employee orientation program this year. A major step in accomplishing this goal might be to evaluate and update the current orientation materials. This major step might require several weeks.

ACTIVITIES AND TASKS

Once you have major steps identified for each of your goals, you need to further break down each major step into a series of smaller activities and tasks. Continuing with the previous example, it might involve four smaller activities and tasks such as: (1) evaluate and revise content; (2) design new orientation materials to match your company brand; (3) print the new materials; and (4) create individual employee orientation packets. Each activity or task is something that can usually be completed in a few hours or over the course of a few days.

IDENTIFY RESOURCES NEEDED

Next, you will need to decide what resources are required to accomplish each activity and task. You might need physical resources such as paper, equipment and storage facilities. You might need financial resources such as cash or a line of credit. You might need human resources such as people with specific skill sets or specific roles to play. You might also need resources outside your company, such as a printing company and a graphic designer.

PERSON(S) RESPONSIBLE

Chances are that many people will be working toward the same goals. So, you need to determine who should be responsible for each activity and task in the action plan. Assigning responsibility to someone doesn't necessarily mean that person will do every task. It just means that person will make sure the tasks get done, even if he or she doesn't personally do them. As you assign responsibility, you might want to consider everyone's abilities, passions, authority and sense of ownership. For example, don't assign design responsibilities to someone who doesn't know what good design is. Likewise, if someone is passionate about a specific step in the plan, you might want to ask that person to oversee that part of the process.

SET DEADLINES

Finally, set deadlines for each major step, activities and tasks. As you establish deadlines, you might think about the sequence or flow of the overall plan. What major steps need to happen first? What should happen last? What activities need to be completed before you can start other activities? For example, you can't print materials until they have been written.

You should also consider the availability of the people working on the plan. When are they available to accomplish specific tasks or activities? Budget your time wisely. Think about how much time is realistically needed to perform each activity and task. If you allow too much time, people will procrastinate. If you allow too little time, you might end up with frustrated employees.

In the next chapter, we will examine the final step in the strategic planning process: evaluation. Evaluation adds the important element of accountability to the strategic planning process.

CHAPTER TEN

Step 5: Evaluation

Measure what is measurable, and make measurable what is not so.

Attributed to Galileo

American pop psychologist Dr. Phil is best known for his nationally televised talk show where people discuss their problems with him. The show focuses on uncovering the strategies (often bad ones) that his guests use to solve their problems. Inevitably, at some point during the show, Dr. Phil will pause and ask, "And how's that working out for you?" The question is designed to stop people in their tracks and force them to evaluate their strategies in light of reality. All plans sound great on paper, but many don't look so great in the real world.

Having a strategic plan doesn't automatically translate into great results. Circumstances change and new challenges arise after plans have been carefully made. Life throws curve balls and it's easy to lose focus. Therefore, Dr. Phil's question is an appropriate one to ask as you work toward implementing your strategic plan. "How's that working out for you?" You should be willing to ask the tough questions about your plans if you want to make sure that you are actually moving toward your vision. Establishing a set of metrics is a good place to start in creating a healthy evaluation process.

WHAT TO EVALUATE?

The first step in evaluating any strategy is to ask, "What are you evaluating?" To answer this question, you need to establish a strategic metric. This is a standard and a process of measuring and evaluating your goals.

The specific things that you plan to evaluate are often referred to as metric indicators.

Think of metric indicators as gauges on your car. A car has a gasoline (petrol) gauge to evaluate how much gasoline is available. It has a speedometer to evaluate how fast the car is traveling and a mileage counter to evaluate how far the car has traveled. There are also gauges to monitor the engine temperature and engine oil levels.

While there are a number of gauges that supply useful measurements, car makers could have added many others. They could have included gauges to assess the amount of oxygen in the air or the barometric pressure inside the car. They could have also added gauges to measure the amount of ultraviolet light coming through the windshield or the surface temperature of the roof. No doubt, there are countless gauges they could have included. But they didn't. Instead, car makers have chosen to include only a limited number of gauges that provide information that is critical for drivers to know. The other unnecessary gauges would actually distract the driver from that critical information. Likewise you should determine what not to evaluate in your strategic plan. You should only evaluate the critical aspects of your plan so that you don't become distracted by too much information.

There is no one-size-fits-all set of gauges (strategic metrics). A business strategic plan might include financial metric indicators to measure sales numbers, profits, or expenses. Nonprofit organizations might have some gauges to measure social or environmental impact in the communities they serve. A hospital might want to measure patient recovery rates, quality of care and reduction rates of communicable infections. Factories might want to track employee safety records, production quality and production speed.

Business professors and strategy consultants Robert S Kaplan and David P Norton recognized that most organizations have multiple bottom lines. Although financial measurements are important, they are just one way of gauging the health of an organizational strategy. Other categories that Kaplan and Norton suggest include aspects like employee satisfaction, customer growth, structural efficiency and organizational learning.

As I've said, there is no generic set of gauges. A simple rule of thumb is that your metric indicators should align with your goals. If your goal is to make some sort of impact in society, but you are evaluating your accounting systems, you are not using the right set of indicators. If your goal is focused on improving customer service, but you are measuring employee safety records, your metric is not aligned with your goal.

HOW TO EVALUATE?

Once you've determined what you need to evaluate, you'll need to determine how to go about evaluating it. You don't measure gasoline levels, vehicle speed and engine temperature in the same way. Knowing the current velocity of your car won't tell you if you have enough gasoline to make it to the next city. Likewise, different strategic goals require different methods of measurement. There are three basic methods to measure: raw data, progress and benchmarks.

Raw Data

First, you can measure the raw data. Raw data is like a gasoline gauge. It tells you how much gasoline is in the tank. Examples of raw data measurements might include: How much revenue did we generate this quarter? How many people were impacted by our project? How many people did our marketing plan reach? Just as your gasoline gauge can't tell you how long it might take to get to the next city, raw data doesn't really tell how long it might take to achieve your goal. For that you need to measure progress.

Progress

Progress is like a mileage counter. A mileage counter can be set to zero at the start of a trip. Then, it will measure the distance you've traveled. By doing so, it will also tell you what progress you've made toward your destination. Likewise, you can measure how far toward a particular goal you have come. Most goals are not binary. If your personal goal is to lose 10 kilos and you only lost 9 kilos, you wouldn't say that you failed to achieve your goal. A more accurate assessment would be to say that you accomplished 90% of your goal.

Progress metrics can also help you determine how long it might take to achieve a particular goal. In a sense progress metrics are like a mileage counter and a speedometer. The mileage counter tells you how far you've traveled. You can use that information to calculate how much distance you have left to travel. The speedometer tells you how fast you are traveling. That can help you predict if you will make it to your destination in a few minutes or in a few hours. In the same way, you can measure how long it takes to make progress toward your goals. This knowledge can help you predict when you might be able to achieve your goals. Let's use the weight loss goal again, as an example. If it took you 9 months to lose nine kilograms, then you can predict that it might take one more month to lose that final kilogram.

Benchmarks

Lastly, you can set and track major benchmarks (or milestones). If you are planning a long road trip, say from Los Angeles to New York City, you might break it up into several legs. The first leg might be from Los Angeles to Las Vegas. The second leg might be from Las Vegas to Denver and so on. In the same way, a really big goal might be broken up into a series of implementation phases or benchmarks. Once you have established benchmarks, you can measure by checking off each one as you achieve it.

Benchmarks are similar to progress metrics. Both measure movement toward the goal. However, benchmarks aren't usually translated into percentages like progress metrics. Rather, benchmarks measure the completion of major achievements. Some achievements might take longer to pursue than others. The travel time between Los Angeles and Las Vegas isn't the same as between Las Vegas and Denver. Benchmarks say, "We made if from Las Vegas to Denver. Now it's time to go out for a meal and enjoy being in Denver before we hit the road again tomorrow morning."

How Often to Evaluate?

The last piece of the evaluation process is frequency, how often you will evaluate your strategic metrics. Many businesses measure their financials quarterly. However, if you have set a goal to increase monthly sales by 2%, it might be helpful to measure your sales numbers every month rather than quarterly. If you have started a 12-week weight loss plan, you might want to measure your weight at least once a week. You can take measurements daily, weekly, monthly, bi-monthly, or quarterly. If you are not measuring your indicators at least quarterly, then you probably aren't measuring often enough.

That being said, there is no magic number for how often you should evaluate. It all depends on what you are measuring and how you are measuring it. Some measurements are easy to perform daily, like stepping on a bathroom scale. Other measurements would be impossible to measure daily due to the amount of time needed to perform the measurement. A quarterly financial report might take several days to prepare. So, it would not be something you'd want to prepare every week. The rule of thumb is to determine how frequently to measure in light of feasibility and usefulness. If it takes you three days to perform a measurement, you can't feasibly do it every day. However, measuring your finances only once a year will not provide information needed for corrective actions throughout the year.

Now that we have covered the last step in the strategic planning process, we will turn our attention to two practical considerations before concluding this book: execution and collaboration.

SECTION 3:
PRACTICAL CONSIDERATIONS

Nothing ever becomes real till it is experienced.

John Keats

People, trust, buy-in, workflow and organizational culture significantly impact how strategies are implemented. The implementation of a strategy is commonly referred to as execution in business circles. So, I use that term as we explore the factors involved in working out your strategy in the real world. But, I want to clarify that when I talk about execution, I'm talking about implementing strategy rather than electric chairs and firing squads. Equally important is the significant role collaboration plays in strategic planning and execution. Consequently, we will reflect on what collaboration is and is not. Specifically, we will explore what collaboration looks like in terms of labor, resources and decisions.

CHAPTER ELEVEN

Execution

In its most fundamental sense, execution is a systematic way of exposing reality and acting on it.

Larry Bossidy and Ram Charan

Developing a strategy can happen over a relatively short period of time with a relatively small number of people. However, executing a strategy takes place over a long period of time with a much larger number of people depending on the size of the organization. Executive Vice President Randy Ottinger of Kotter International explains, "When we consider the strategy in whole, a minority of effort and resources is invested to develop a strategy (maybe 10%). The real work (maybe 90%) of the effort and resources is required to execute the strategy" (Forbes, 2012).

Strategic planning is the easy part. Execution is the difficult part. It's also the most important part of a successful strategy. That just makes sense doesn't it? What good is an incredible strategy if it never gets executed or is executed so poorly that it fails miserably? Harvard Business Researcher John Kotter found that "70% of the strategic change efforts fail because of how people go about executing those strategies" (Forbes, 2012). In many cases, the strategic plans were excellent. The breakdown happened in the implementation of those plans in the real world.

One challenge of execution is the shift from planning to doing. Planning is relatively risk free and certainly less exhausting. Let's put this in terms of exercise. Creating a fitness plan is a relatively painless activity. In fact, you can download a professionally designed plan in seconds from hundreds of online fitness gurus. The real challenge happens when you shift from planning to actually doing 25 push-ups everyday. You won't injure yourself by planning to run a marathon. When you hit the streets, though, you run the risk of pulling a hamstring. You can sit by a warm and cozy fire and plan to swim ten laps. It's the 6:00 a.m. plunge in the pool that sends a freezing shock through your system.

The gap between planning and doing can create a sense of paralysis. Sometime, people get stuck in the gap. In many cases, they end up going back to the plan over and over again to "refine" it. They say things like, "Well, 25 push-ups is too many to start with. I'll shoot for 20 instead. No wait, I've got a bad shoulder. Perhaps I should try jumping jacks . . ." On and on they go, ever planning, never doing.

Another difficulty in the process of execution is getting people to work together. Planning for people to work together toward a shared vision is a fairly straightforward activity. Actually coordinating the efforts of people across an organization can be quite challenging and complicated. Nielson, Martin and Powers have noted in the Harvard Business Review that "Execution is the result of thousands of decisions made every day by employees acting according to the information they have and their own self-interest" (HBR, 2011).

Think for a moment about executing the simple goal of "increasing sales by 10%" in a typical manufacturing company. This goal requires the conscious efforts of the entire sales team to push themselves harder every day to make a few extra sales. It requires the marketing team to develop a plan to reach new customers. It requires customer service representatives to make an increased volume of phone calls to new customers. It requires the factory crew to increase their output in order to meet the new demand without compromising quality. It requires that the administrative staff ensure that adequate supplies are ordered on time to keep up with the increased production. The order fulfillment department must ramp up its efforts to get the increased orders shipped to customers on time. Managers across the company need to coordinate resources to make it all happen.

Execution also requires discipline and focus. One of the keys to effective execution is knowing where to invest your time, people and resource and then being consistent in making that investment. Often the discipline of saying "no" is involved. Strategy researcher Michael Porter says, "the essence of strategy is choosing what not to do" (HBR, 1996). There are a lot of good things you could do while executing your strategy. However, good things can distract you from the important things. You need to focus on the important things and let the other things go undone.

THE COMPONENTS OF EXECUTION

There are a number of key components involved in effectively executing a strategic plan. Entire books have been written on the subject of execution, including Larry Bossidy and Ram Charan's classic Execution: The Discipline of Getting Things Done and The 4 Disciplines of Execution: Achieving Your Wildly Important Goals by Chris McChesney, Sean Covey and Jim Huling. Therefore, what follows merely scratches the surface on this topic.

Buy-in

Any strategy that depends on the efforts of other people is going to require their buy-in. If the people responsible for implementing the strategy are not internally motivated and inspired by the strategy, you will end up with mediocre execution at best and complete failure at worst. Compelling vision is critical to strategy.

I will never forget the new employee orientation at an international school where I worked for a few years in Hanoi. I remember it vividly, not because it was so inspiring, but because it was just the opposite. The keynote address of the day came from the CEO of the company that owned this particular international school. He stood before the crowded room of professional educators and said, "I want you to clearly understand that our bottom line is not students. It's not parents. It's not the curriculum. And, it's certainly not the teachers. Our bottom line is the shareholder. We are a business and we are here to make a profit." The teachers in the room looked at each another in complete shock. I didn't speak to everyone there, but I'm pretty sure not a single teacher there cared one bit about the pockets of the shareholders. Needless to say, the organization had very little buy-in when it rolled out new strategic initiatives each year for increasing profits.

Get-Stuff-Done Culture

Once you have buy-in, you need to create a culture within your organization that is focused on action, on getting stuff done. There needs to be a sense of urgency surrounding your strategy. One of the best ways to create this culture is by modeling it. Nobody likes leaders who sit around all day barking orders. People are inspired to act when they see leaders leading by example. When leaders get stuff done, it creates followers who get stuff done. There is a place for delegation, and successful execution depends on delegating the right things to the right people. But if leaders always delegate and never dive in and get their hands dirty, others will feel more like mules than people. It could also promote the idea that delegation is the focus rather than action. But, if everybody is delegating, who's actually getting stuff done?

Trust

Patrick Lencioni has eloquently noted in his bestselling book, The Five Dysfunctions of a Team, that trust is the foundation of a healthy team. In his book, he goes on to teach that an absence of trust creates a fear of conflict. If people are afraid of conflict, they will not share their ideas and engage in constructive debate. If they don't share their ideas, there will be a lack of consensus and lack of commitment (buy-in). If there is a lack of commitment, people will avoid accountability, and that will produce an organizational culture that is not concerned with results. The point of his book is that if you want to see results, if you want to execute a strategy effectively, then you need to develop an atmosphere of trust.

The Right People in the Right Place

Bestselling business author Jim Collins suggests that it is critical to get the right people on the bus and then have them sit in the right seats. His metaphor highlights the importance of people in the process of executing a strategy. As you assign people to oversee and implement various parts of the strategy, the key is to find the right people. It is assumed that you know your people well enough to assign them properly. Don't just assign people at random. Try to match each part of the strategy with people who have the right mix of skills, passion and strengths to execute it well.

A Workflow System

Execution is a systematized process of achieving your strategic goals. Therefore, you need to translate your strategic goals and action plan into an everyday flow of work. Let's think about learning a new language to illustrate this point. If you want to learn a new language, you will need to translate that goal into a set of workflow rhythms. You can't cram language learning. It requires doing a set of daily and weekly language learning activities. For example, you might want to practice speaking with and listening to a native speaker at least once a day. You might also set aside time every week to review new vocabulary that you are learning.

Iteration

Strategy is an organic process. John Lennon said, "Life is what happens while you're busy making other plans." His point is that you really can't plan for every possible thing that could happen. Life seems to always find a way to throw monkey wrenches into our plans. If your strategy is seen as something inorganic and set in stone, it might not fit reality so well. Therefore, as you begin executing your plans, be prepared to iterate as you go.

If unforeseen circumstances arise that you couldn't plan for ahead of time, then you need to adjust your strategy. Please don't misunderstand. I'm not advocating that you change your goals to make them easier once life gets difficult. Rather, I'm simply saying that we need to adjust our strategies as they unfold in light of reality. In some cases it might even involve making your goals more ambitious than planned.

This is exactly how strategy works in chess. You might have a set of plays in your head (your strategy) that you are ready to execute. Then your opponent makes a move that renders that set of plays absolutely useless. What do you do? You pivot your strategy to match the current situation. If fact, if you ignore reality and keep to your original plan, you wouldn't be very strategic at all. Successful execution requires iteration.

Aligned Process and Resources

Effective execution of a strategy depends on having your organizational processes and resources aligned with your strategy. Every person should have the information they need to execute the tasks assigned to them. In many cases, people must be empowered with decision-making authority (and boundaries) to move forward. Micromanaging a strategy never works out well. Instead, it congests the workflow and demotivates people.

Make sure that the resources required to execute the strategy are available as well. This doesn't mean that you need to have all the resources available when you launch your strategy. But, those resources must be available when they are needed as the strategy unfolds.

Clear and Regular Communication

Information needs to flow freely across the organization. Transparency is critical. The more that people are left in the dark or have to guess, the less effective they become at execution. Some key pieces of information include decisions and responsibility. Everyone should clearly understand critical decisions and any tasks for which they are responsible. One major complaint against management is the lack of clarity about job expectations.

Communication also needs to happen regularly. Many teams have found that a daily five-minute check-in or huddle works well to: regularly gauge current status; agree on today's priorities; and determine if anyone needs assistance or additional resources. Longer meetings can be held weekly or every few weeks to discuss and evaluate bigger issues involved in executing the strategy.

Consistent Tracking of Results

Finally, great execution requires a consistent focus on results. However, don't make the mistake of using results as a weapon against your team. You want to push everyone toward your strategic goals, but you don't want to push them off a cliff. Sometimes, passion for results can feel like slave driving to those at the other end of the whip. You need to learn how to push without coming across as a slave driver. There are a few ways this can be done.

Celebrating small wins and milestones is a positive way to demonstrate a passion for results that motivate people to achieve more. Rewarding and recognizing people for completing important tasks also goes a long way toward keeping them focused on moving forward. You can use coaching techniques to empower and motivate people as well. Coaching focuses on drawing passion out of people by asking good questions that help connect people's passions with the work that needs to be done.

When all is said and done, people are the most critical component of a well-executed strategy. Successful execution hinges on people working well together. Collaboration is the art of people working together in a way that multiplies their efforts and creates something special that could never be created alone. Therefore, let's turn our attention now to the skill of collaboration.

CHAPTER TWELVE

Collaboration

When I was a kid, there was no collaboration; it's you with a camera bossing your friends around. But as an adult, filmmaking is all about appreciating the talents of the people you surround yourself with and knowing you could never have made any of these films by yourself.

Steven Spielberg

Collaboration can be messy, but powerful. It's much easier to be directive if you just want to get things done. However, if you want to do great things, collaboration is vital. Visionary companies like Apple rely on collaboration to consistently create wildly successful products. Steve Jobs explained that Apple wanted "to develop integrated products, and that meant our process had to be integrated and collaborative." He went on to say that there were "zero committees at Apple. We are organized like a startup. It's the biggest startup on the planet and we all meet for three hours a week to talk about everything we're doing, the whole business." He passionately believed that exceptional collaboration at the executive level of Apple would set an ex-ample and filter down to exceptional collaboration throughout the entire organization.

COLLABORATION IS NOT CONSULTATION

What is collaboration? Let's begin by identifying what collaboration is not. Collaboration is not consultation. Consultation is the process of gathering information, suggestions and advice from others and then making unilater-al decisions and actions based on that information, suggestions and advice. In a consultative process, most people play the role of advisors. Though their ideas are heard and considered, at the end of the day, important decisions are top-down. One person (or a very small group) sets the strategic goals on behalf of the entire team or organization. Likewise, work is delegated and resources are allocated from the top down. This is not bad if your goal is simply management operational processes. Getting feedback from people in the process through consultation is helpful for fine-tuning how to manage things.

COLLABORATION IS NOT COOPERATION

Collaboration is also not the same as cooperation which is working together in a way that is mutually advantageous to all parties. Cooperation involves a division of labor to get things done. However, what needs to be done is by and large a conglomeration of the tasks of individuals. The mentality is, "I'll scratch your back if you scratch mine." Instead of competing for resources, people share resources so that everyone can benefit. Decisions are often a democratic process that appeals to the majority of individual opinions. Thus, decisions are pragmatic, based on what benefits most people.

WHAT COLLABORATION IS

 The chart in Figure 10 compares collaboration with consultation and cooperation. Regarding labor, collaboration seeks to synchronize work in order to complete shared strategic goals rather than delegating labor from the top down or dividing labor for the mutual benefit of individual goals. Resources are not shared equally, but are coordinated toward the benefit of mutual objectives. In a collaborative environment, decisions are not unilateral (based on advice) or democratic (for the benefit of most). Rather, decisions are communal and flow out of commitment to a shared vision. Collaborative decisions allow several people to take part in the decision-making process. The goal is to make decisions based on what is best for the shared vision, not what is best for most people. Sometimes what is best for most people is also best for the shared vision, but that isn't always the case.

	CONSULTATION	COOPERATION	COLLABORATION
LABOR	Delegated	Divided	Synchronized
RESOURCES	Allocated	Shared for mutual benefit	Coordinated toward mutual objectives
DECISIONS	Advisory	Democratic	Communal Vision

Figure 10: Consultation, Cooperation and Collaboration Chart

The quote from Stephen Spielberg at the beginning of this chapter highlights the fact that doing great things requires collaboration. Dictators do not make films (at least not good ones). Directors make films. A director might come to a scene with a general idea of where it needs to go. But, the actors bring to each scene their interpretations of the characters' dialogue and actions. The camera crew comes with their ideas for how to capture the scene on film. The lighting crew thinks through the best way to light the scene so that it adds to the action and helps it to look good on film. The sound crew decides what natural sounds to use and which sound effects to apply. Composers create music to match the mood of the scene. Costume designers dress the actors in clothing that fits the time period, setting and the individual characters. The special effects (FX) team determines which types of special effects are needed and how to make them. All of these people are working with each other to make sure each scene is the best it can possibly be.

TECHNOLOGY IS A TOOL

There are some amazing collaboration tools today. Many of these tools are inexpensive and even free including: Google Apps, Trello and Skype. But we need to recognize that, although technology offers some incredible tools for collaboration, technology is not collaboration. Let me say that again. Technology is not collaboration. It can greatly enhance collaboration, but it isn't collaboration. Collaboration happens when two are more people work together to achieve or create something they can't do alone.

Sharing a Google Doc with others to show people the strategic plan that you've created isn't collaboration. However, working together to write a strategic plan using a shared Google Doc is collaboration. If you use Trello to merely delegate tasks to other people, you are not engaging in collaboration. But if you and your colleagues build a project task list by working together on Trello, then you are collaborating. Hosting a Skype call to inform your team about the decisions you've made isn't collaboration. Hosting a Skype call to make decisions together is collaboration.

COLLABORATION IS A SYSTEM

Everything and everyone is connected. We might build silos to keep our work clearly separated from others' work. However, reality doesn't operate in silos. Reality is made up of complex systems. Senior Lecturer at MIT's Sloan School of Management Peter Senge applied the idea of systems to organizational behavior. He explained, "Systems thinking is a discipline for seeing wholes. It is a framework for seeing interrelationships rather than things, for seeing patterns of change rather than static snapshots."

Let's think about a car. Every part of the car is connected and affects all the other car parts. If I want to increase the speed, I need to press down on the accelerator. As I press down, the pedal pulls a cable that is connected to the acceleration system in the motor. The acceleration system sends more fuel to the motor causing an increase in the axle's revolutions per minute (RPMs). The axle is connected to the wheels causing them to spin faster, thus increasing the speed of the car. But, that's not all. If I don't have the key in the ignition and if the engine isn't turned on, I can push the accelerator pedal all I want without any result. If there is no fuel in the fuel tank, the car won't even start. If I have the emergency brake on while trying to accelerate, my speed and rate of acceleration will be adversely impacted. If the car is pulling a trailer, the trailer will also affect the acceleration. Even having the car windows up or down impacts the acceleration rate.

As we apply this idea to collaboration, we recognize that our decisions and actions impact everything and everyone on our team and in our organization. Collaboration isn't just working well together. Effective collaboration asks people to work together as an organized system, to work together like the parts of a car work together. Collaboration asks people to synchronize their efforts with each other so they can accomplish something that could not be possible by working in silos.

When you collaborate, you aren't just concerned with completing the tasks assigned to you. Rather, you are concerned with how your tasks advance or impede the workflow of others. You see your work in the context of the overall strategy. You make decisions about your work based on how it will impact the whole, not just the parts. How will completing a particular task today versus tomorrow impact the workflow of the entire organization? How will time spent filling out paperwork impact time spent with customers? How will my department's budget impact the budgets of other departments? How will sales targets impact the production team? These are the types of questions to ask as you engage in collaboration.

SYMPHONIES AND CONSTRUCTION CREWS

Sometimes collaboration works like a symphony and other times it's like a construction crew. Symphonies involve a group of people playing different instruments at the same time in sync with each other. The result of a well-orchestrated symphony is a beautiful piece of music that no musician could perform alone. The key idea here is that everyone is working together at the same time. The film crew is a collaborative symphony. The director, actors, sound crew, FX team, camera operators, lighting crew and many others are working together at the same time to film a scene.

A construction crew is similar to a symphony orchestra in that each involves a group of people coming together through synchronized efforts to create something that no single person could create on their own. However, construction crews don't work together at the same time. In fact, most of the time they can't work together at the same time, because their work is often sequential. A survey team comes out first to analyze the land. Then, another crew comes along to lay the foundation. Once the foundation is laid, framers build the walls and roof. Next, come the plumbers, electricians, a drywall crew and flooring team. Finally, painters add color to the bare walls and roofers lay shingles on the rooftop.

Though the work doesn't happen at the same time, it does need to be synchronized. If the foundation-laying crew pours the wrong dimensions for the foundation, the entire building project will be affected. The framers need a basic idea of where the plumbing and electricity will be in order to build the walls correctly. Each crew in the construction process needs to think about the work of the other crews if the house is to pass inspection.

Likewise, some aspects of a strategy might require sequential collaboration. For example, a nonprofit's strategy to provide clean water to one hundred villages in one year might begin with the work of a team of fundraisers. Once sufficient funds are raised, the nonprofit can hire a team of engineers to design affordable water wells. After that, they can recruit a group of local volunteers to install the water wells in each village and teach inhabitants how to maintain the wells. The local villagers can't build the wells until the engineers provide accurate designs. And nothing can get started until sufficient funds are in place to hire the engineers and purchase the supplies.

At the end of the day, collaboration is an effective tool for most of what is involved in strategic planning and execution. However, before concluding this chapter, I must admit that collaboration isn't required for every detail in a successful strategy. If fact, collaboration can be cumbersome for many mundane tasks. Some elements of a strategy might be better-suited to quick top-down decisions and actions. For example, deciding which printing company to use for a marketing piece shouldn't require a collaborative team discussion. Likewise, simple cooperation might be sufficient for other parts of a strategy that don't depend on synchronized efforts and resources. The use of a copy machine (as a shared resource) rarely needs to be synchronized by a collaborative committee. A simple system for sharing the machine is usually sufficient. In fact, most large copy machines have built in queuing software that does the sharing work for you.

A general rule of thumb for when to collaborate involves scope. The broader the scope, the greater is the need for collaboration. Anything that will impact several people on the team should be done collaboratively. Likewise, anything that requires the efforts of several people should be done collaboratively. Collaboration should also be used for anything that has a major impact (negative or positive) on the entire system or strategy.

CHAPTER THIRTEEN

Conclusion

To begin, begin.

William Wordsworth

You've reached the final chapter. Now what? I could restate everything in a neat little summary chapter, but that seems like a waste of space. Instead, I'll challenge you to go out and work on creating a strategy. There's no better way to learn than by getting started. To help you out, I'll conclude this book with a suggested schedule and agenda for a two-day strategy retreat for your team.

PREPARATION FOR STRATEGY RETREAT

The Venue

It's best to choose an offsite venue for the retreat. Holding it at the work-place can be distracting. Clients and staff interrupt the flow of the discussions. The office will constantly remind everyone of the work that is crying out for attention, and your people will be tempted to get a few things done between sessions.

You don't need to travel far or spend a lot of money. However, try to choose a place that is refreshing for your team. It can be at an uncle's cabin, a friend's timeshare, a mid-range hotel or a vacation home rental. If you are able to schedule your retreat during the off-season, you can usually find great deals at nice resorts. Where you go isn't as important as getting out of the office.

If possible, try to stay overnight to allow for informal connecting and conversations. During downtimes our brains are still working and processing the formal discussions. Some of the best ideas and breakthroughs come to people during those informal downtimes.

The Participants

Decide beforehand who should participate in the retreat. You will obviously want your key leaders to attend. However, are there other stakeholders whose voice and ideas would be beneficial? Perhaps a board member or an important partner in the community would be helpful? You might also consider inviting people who can help the retreat run smoothly such as an administrative staff person to keep notes and act as a liaison with the venue. A skilled retreat facilitator can also keep discussions moving forward and keep the group from going down too many rabbit trails.

The Homework

Give everyone a copy of this book and ask them to read at least chapters four through ten prior to the retreat. This will bring everyone up to speed on the five steps in the strategic planning process and give them a basic idea of the agenda for the retreat. You could even schedule a short meeting at the office to give a brief overview of the five steps of the process.

As you begin the retreat, you will spend time developing your vision, revising your vision or simply reviewing your vision. Therefore, ask everyone to personally interact regarding the team's vision prior to the retreat. If you already have a developed vision, send it to the retreat participants and ask them to come prepared to share what is personally inspiring about the vision. If you don't have a vision, ask participants to think about your team, project or organization ten years from now. Ask them to come prepared to share what the future could look like in ten years.

DAY ONE

Session 1: Vision (1 hour)

- Video (10-15 minutes): Watch an inspiring video about vision such as Martin Luther King, Jr.'s "I Have a Dream" speech (available on YouTube) or another video that is relevant to your project or organization.

- Personal Response (5 minutes): Ask each participant to dream about the future of your team, project or organization. Instruct them to jot down notes about what the future could look like for your team, project or organization. If you already have a vision, ask participants to jot down what inspires them about the current vision. This shouldn't take long since you've asked participants to think about this prior to the retreat.

- Small Groups (20 minutes): Break up into small groups of three to five people. Each person will share his/her personal response, and then the group will identify shared ideas from the individual responses. Elect someone to record the shared ideas.

- Whole Group (20 minutes): Each group will share a summary of their ideas. Then the group will try to combine ideas generated in the small groups into a shared vision (unless you already have a vision). Drafting a beautiful statement isn't the goal. Seeing a shared vision is.

Break (10-15 minutes)

Session 2: SWOT Analysis (1 hour)

- Set-up (5 minutes): Explain what a SWOT analysis is (see Chapter 5). Position four large flipcharts in each corner of the room. Label each chart for a quadrant of the SWOT analysis (or use the boat-anchor-island-iceberg metaphors from Chapter 5).

- Sticky-note Response (15 minutes): Distribute pens and four sticky-note pads (of different colors) to each person. Ask participants to write down strengths on individual yellow sticky notes and post them on the flipchart labeled "Strengths." Do the same with the other colors for weaknesses, opportunities and threats. Encourage people to move around the room as they do this activity. They can start with any category and return to any category as often as they want during the exercise.

- Review (40 minutes): Take ten minutes per chart to review the findings with the group. Combine similar responses by moving the sticky notes into clusters. Then, ask participants to vote on the top three responses for each category of the SWOT analysis by raising hands. Each person can only vote three times. Make a tick mark on the flipchart next to each response for each vote. Have someone type the four lists into a SWOT analysis document.

Break (15-30 minutes)

During the break, finish typing up the SWOT analysis. It will be needed for the next activity. Distribute a hard or soft copy of the SWOT analysis results to each participant.

Session 3: Seeking Goals (1 hour)

- Working Groups (30 minutes): Break up into working groups of three to five people. Using the SWOT analysis from session 2, generate a list of potential strategic goals (see Chapter 6).

- Whole Group (30 minutes): Each working group shares findings with the entire group. Identify and combine similar potential strategic goals. Generate a new list that represents the whole group. Type the new list in a document to be used for the next session.

Lunch Break (1.5 hours)

Session 4: Sifting Goals (1 hour)

- Working Groups (30 minutes): Break into working groups of three to five people. Using the list of potential goals from session 3 and the filters presented in Chapter 7 identify which goals should be eliminated and pursued. Finally, rank each potential goal that might be worth pursuing.

- Whole Group (30 minutes): Each working group shares ranked potential goals. Identify and combine similar goals and rankings. Vote for three to five goals to focus on this year.

Break (15-30 minutes)

Session 5: Setting Goals (1 hour)

- Whole group: Write one of the strategic goals from the previous session on a whiteboard. Use the questions at the end of Chapter 8 to reword the goal so as to make it a SMAART goal. Repeat this process for each goal.

Day One Downtime

Wrap up discussions and do something social together. Play a board game. Watch a movie. Go out for dinner. Your collective minds have been on overdrive. They need time to be refreshed and renewed. During this downtime, your mind will actually continue to work on the information and discussions. How many times have you been struck by a great idea two hours after a meeting? Downtime gives your brain space to process and sort through everything. You'll be surprised at how many great thoughts just seem to pop into people's minds and social conversations during this down-time.

DAY TWO

Session 1: Opening session (1 hour)

- Highlights and Insights (20-30 minutes): Give participants 5 to 10 minutes to write down 2-3 highlights and 2-3 insights from Day One. Next, go around the room and ask each person to share one highlight and one insight that he/she wrote down. (Note: A high-light is something inspiring or positive. An insight is an ah-ha moment when a cloudy idea become clear, a problem is understood better, or a solution comes into focus.)

- All-In (30 minutes): Give each participant a poker chip (or similar type of token). Review each of the goals that were developed at the end of Day One. Allow a few minutes for discussion and refinement of the goals. Explain to the participants that everyone needs to be all-in (completely supportive of the goals). One by one, go around the room and collect the poker chips. As each person submits his/her poker chip, ask, "Are you all-in on these goals?" This is a great way to symbolize the buy-in of your team.

Break (10-15 minutes)

Session 2: Action (1 hour)

- Work Groups (30 minutes): Break up into small groups (3-5 people). Assign each group the task of developing one goal into an action plan (see Chapter 9 for details).

- Whole Group (30 minutes): Each group shares the details of their action plan and asks for input from the entire group. Make any modification and then vote to accept the action plan.

Break (15-30 minutes)

Session 3: Evaluation (1 hour)

- Work Groups (30 minutes): Gather in the same small groups from session 2. This time each group will develop a set of metrics for their goal and action plan (see Chapter 10 for details). They will determine what to evaluate, how to evaluate and how often to evaluate.

- Whole Group (30 minutes): Each group shares the details of their metrics and obtains input from the whole group. Make any modification and then vote to accept the metrics.

Lunch Break (1.5 hours)

Session 4: Wrap-up (1 hour)

- Review (20-30 minutes): Briefly review each section of the strategic plan you have developed (vision, reality, goals, actions and evaluation). Ask for further comments and feedback as you review each section.

- Calendars (20-30 minutes): Pull out your calendars and schedule the first steps in the implementation of the strategy and set a date for your first major strategic evaluation.

I recommend making strategic planning an annual workflow rhythm for your organization or team. Choose a time near the start of your yearly organizational cycle (calendar year, fiscal year or academic year, whatever is most practical). If you are feeling uncertain about going through the process alone, we can walk your team through it. Visit *www.navseries.com* to learn more.

Now, put the book down and go create a strategy!

Selected Bibliography

Bossidy, L., Charan, R., & Burck, C. (2011). *Execution: the discipline of getting things done.* London: Random House Business Books.

Collins, J. (2001). *Good to great: Why some companies make the leap . . . and others don't.* Harper Business.

Kaplan, R. S., & Norton, D. P. (1996). *The balanced scorecard: translating strategy into action.* Boston, MA: Harvard Business School Press.

Kim, W. C., & Mauborgne, R. (2016). *Blue ocean strategy: how to create uncontested market space and make the competition irrelevant.* Boston, Massachusetts: Harvard Bus Review Press.

Leinwand, P., & Mainardi, C. R. (2016). *Strategy that works: how winning companies close the strategy-to-execution gap.* Boston: Harvard Business Review Press.

McChesney, C., Covey, S., & Huling, J. (2016). *The 4 disciplines of execution: achieving your wildly important goals.* New York: Free Press.

Neilson, G. L., Martin, K. L., and Powers, E. (2008) *The secrets to successful strategy execution.* Harvard Business Review (June): 60-71.

Porter, M. E. (2008). *The five competitive forces that shape strategy.* Harvard Business Review (January): 1-17.

Porter, M. E. (1996). *What is a strategy?* Harvard Business Review (November-December): 61-78.

Senge, P. M. (1990). *The fifth discipline: the art and practice of the learning organization.* New York: Doubleday.

NAVIGATING Business Series

Other Navigating Business topics include:

STRATEGY	DESIGN	LEADERSHIP
CULTURES	BRANDING	TEAMS
TRANSITIONS	MESSAGING	CONFLICT

The NAVIGATING Business Series has grown out of decades of experience in small business development and cross-cultural work spanning North America, Central Asia, Southeast Asia and Africa. Our leadership team has combined their knowledge and expertise to bring you practical insights and principles that can be applied to a multitude of marketplace challenges.

Visit *www.navseries.com* and *www.simplegroupglobal.com* to learn more.

About the Author

Michael W. Beard has worked in Asia for about 20 years and holds a masters degree in Intercultural Studies. While living in Kyrgyzstan (Central Asia), he helped to launch a business training and incubation center where local entrepreneurs learned to run small businesses through mentoring and hands-on experience. He also has a background in education from primary school to university and has created the content for several topics in the Navigating Business Series with Simple Group Global. Michael is a Partner and Chief Operating Officer of Simple Group Global. He and his wife Michelle live in Vietnam and have four adult children.

www.ingramcontent.com/pod-product-compliance
Lightning Source LLC
Chambersburg PA
CBHW050511210326
41521CB00011B/2407